Testimonials

This is a truly original and thought-prov̶ [...] recommend it to the federal government's ca.... managers, who are greatly in need of a pick-me-up as well as a dose of fresh thinking.

–Marilena Amoni, retired Associate Administrator, National Highway Traffic Safety Administration, U.S. Department of Transportation

A thoughtful analysis that should be a must read for any elected or appointed official–or anyone contemplating such a career.

–John Laird, Secretary of Natural Resources and former Assemblymember, State of California

I wish every elected official and career manager would read this wonderful book. There is no "same old" to be found here. The author's prescriptions would reshape and revitalize the institutions of government.

–Bruce A. McPherson, former Secretary of State, Senator, and Assemblymember, State of California

Anyone interested in how government actually works, and how it could work better, would be wise to pay careful attention to this path-breaking work. Wilson offers surprising and stunning insights. It is destined to become a classic in schools of public administration.

–Michael Rotkin, Ph.D., retired Lecturer and Director of Field Studies, Department of Community Studies, University of California, Santa Cruz; five-time Mayor and six-term City Councilmember, City of Santa Cruz, California

The author presents a compelling, clear, and practical discussion of political and managerial values and roles in the public sector – a "must read" for elected officials, public managers, academics, and students.

–Les White, retired city manager of San Jose and Fullerton, California

Rethinking
Public Administration

The Case for Management

RICHARD CLAY
WILSON, JR.

Mill City Press, Minneapolis

Mill City Press, Inc.
322 First Avenue N, 5th floor
Minneapolis, MN 55401
612.455.2294
www.millcitypublishing.com

ISBN-13: 978-1-62652-338-8
LCCN: 2013914349

Cover Design by Sophie Chi
Typeset by Mary Kristin Ross

Printed in the United States of America

WHOLESALERS REMAINDERS COM LLC
742 ANDERSON ROAD NORTH
ROCK; HILL, SC; 29730

W 0.54 Standard   S12.24 P0.84

Shipped to:

Lehman Walker
724 SWARTHMORE LN
SAINT LOUIS, MISSOURI 63130-3618

ISBN / Title

162652338X Qty - 1

Rethinking Public Administration: The Case for Man

If you have received defective or incorrectly shipped merchandise, please notify Customer Service at
(803)327-9028 within 7 days and follow their instructions for returns. Original shipment and handling
charges are not refundable, and you will be responsible for all costs associated with return shipment. No
COD returns will be accepted - Return postage is not included in Media rate shipping. So you CAN NOT just
mark the package Return to sender!

If you need an itemized Receipt you will need to obtain it from your Amazon.com account.

Return Label

From:

Lehman Walker
724 SWARTHMORE LN
SAINT LOUIS, MISSOURI 63130-3618

To: 104-8522074-6574628

Returns/BooKnack
742 ANDERSON ROAD NORTH
Rock Hill, SC 29730

Special Thanks

A large helping of special thanks is due Rob Kaplan, of Cortlandt Manor, New York, who edited the manuscript and produced a greatly improved product. The downside of working with an editor of Rob's caliber, of course, is that shortcomings are clearly attributable to the author.
I also wish to thank Suzanne Haberman for her methodical review of and corrections to the print-ready manuscript.

A Note to Colleagues

My colleagues in the management endeavor over thirty-eight years contributed to this book in more ways than I could possibly credit. There are too many to name, and if I tried I would forget someone who didn't deserve omission.
A heartfelt "thank you" to all seems better.

Contents

Contents

Preface

It was my good fortune thirty-five years ago to attend a day-long program by Peter Drucker, who will probably always be regarded as the leading thinker and writer about management. He called it "How to Manage Your Boss," which attracted a large audience, but he actually spent the day guiding participants in thinking through the responsibilities and burdens of their bosses. By the end of the day attendees weren't so sure they knew better than their bosses after all.

That day with Peter Drucker led me to read his books and ask myself how he might think about the experiences I was having in government. When I couldn't figure out what was going on, which was a fair proportion of the time, I did my best to apply Drucker's lenses. I comforted myself that my developing perspectives, whatever their merits, were grounded in Drucker's focus on outcomes. My interest in Drucker also led me to seek managerial wisdom elsewhere.

I spent thirty-eight years in local government. From this vantage point I watched the performance of state and federal officials, elected and career, and noted the results that were in the end visited on the local level. At the same time I was a participant in the drama of local government, and experienced my share of successes and failures.

This book is the product of my experiences and quest to understand. City managers are pragmatists above all other things. Whatever idealism they may start with is quickly extinguished. They are at the mercy of political and other forces beyond their control, as are government's top managers at all levels. I looked for guidance and understanding everywhere, but found less than I needed and hoped for. So I crafted my own conceptions, which are altogether different from those commonly presented.

Government's career managers are much underrated and underequipped. Nevertheless, the future of government will, to a great extent, be the future of its management. Almost no one except government's own managers knows this. I have written this book in the hope of making a small contribution to the understanding of this proposition.

Introduction
The Burden of Indispensability

Imagine, just for the sake of thinking about it, that government has disappeared. Start at the local level. There are no dispatchers to answer 9-1-1 calls, and no police officers or firefighters to respond to them anyway. Local public schools, meaning kindergarten through high school, are closed. The trash is not picked up. Water and sewer treatment plants sit idle. Broken water and sewer mains are not repaired. There is no one to address public hazards, such as faulty bridges or dams. There are no traffic signals. Parks, public bathrooms, and community facilities are unattended. There are no public health authorities, no animal control, and no local courts. Airports are idle. And this list is only the beginning—it is nowhere near complete. It is enough, however, to demonstrate that without the services of the public sector at the local level, our largely civil society would become anything but in just a few hours.

The disappearance of state and federal government would hugely compound the situation. There would be no highway patrol or highway maintenance. Junior colleges, state colleges, and universities would be shuttered. State courts and prisons would be idle. Health and welfare systems would be inoperative. Wildfires would go unattended. Social Security and Medicare payments would be halted. The Defense Department would be shut down, as would other national security agencies. We would retreat from the world as the State Department closed.

These examples are more or less random—I did not cherry-pick them for effect. And these are just a few of the everyday functions of the public sector. The notion that chaos would ensue from the disappearance of government is no exaggeration. As much as we love to malign our government, its existence 24 hours a day and 365 days a year is a prerequisite for normalcy.[1] The very first thing we would have to do if it disappeared would be to re-create it. This is why government is by and large necessary, as are the taxes, fees, and charges that pay for it. This fact of indispensability presents the elected officials who govern essential agencies, and the employees who work for them, with a unique set of responsibilities. From time to time we would do well to ponder them.

In his book, *Capitalism, Socialism, and Democracy*, published in 1942, Joseph Schumpeter famously described capitalism as a process of "creative destruction." A glance at economic history reveals the validity of this insight. Enterprises flourish and fail, some because of their own performance and some due to larger circumstances. And since the majority of our country's employees work for employers that are subject to such randomness, they have no way of knowing if their employers' futures will be long or short. They are simply at risk in that regard. In severe economic downturns such as the one we are now experiencing, the hazards of economic reality become omnipresent.

The indispensable institutions of government, on the other hand, endure, as they must. This is a good thing for the long-term prospects of our economy and society. It is in the nature of things, however, that in the absence of creative destruction the enduring institutions of government sometimes preserve undeserving practices. It follows that, periodically, institutions of government must, in the interest of the public they serve and in their self-interest as well, be willing to change themselves so as to obtain and retain public support for enduring.

More often than not, undeserving practices have to do with the cost of mandatory services and the performance of employees that the public is obliged to employ. Part and parcel of being indispensable and mandatory is the duty to provide services at a reasonable cost and provide competent performance. Less obvious, but of arguably even more consequence, is the duty to structure the multiple layers of government agencies and departments into a coherent whole.

Today's economic circumstances are compelling public agencies everywhere to rethink their fundamental responsibilities and reduce costs. But the economic landscape is not just undergoing a temporary upset—a reordering is underway. This will produce myriad results, many of which are still unknown. We know one of them for sure: tax receipts will be harder to come by. Even in the most optimistic scenarios, public sector employers will find themselves under continuing economic duress. In short, public institutions are experiencing their own form of creative destruction. In such situations the first thing that happens is always the same: organizations learn to function with fewer employees. The private sector "discover(s) who isn't producing very much and fire(s) them."[2] The public sector lays off its most junior employees.

In fact, almost everywhere we look public sector institutions are making unprecedented reductions. Tax receipts for many agencies are still declining in 2012, even if more slowly than before, making further such measures all but certain. And even though many agencies are hard-pressed to find more heads for the chopping block, they will have to do so anyway. It is clear that reducing employment is a necessary step for the institutions of government to take, but it is also clear that doing so is only the beginning in terms of what needs to be done.

The first additional task is to realize structural cost reductions. Economic necessity is the immediate reason to do this, and a long-term reason as well. But an even more important reason is the fundamental obligation to provide mandatory services at a reasonable cost. Public institutions cannot justify a cost platform that has become, in some cases at least, significantly higher than is found in the rest of the economy. This means pay, benefits, pensions, and retiree health care. Reducing these costs would have many benefits, chief among them improving the long-term financial outlook for and public confidence in government institutions.

The second additional task is to remodel the institutions of government. It is well and good to pursue cost-effectiveness one institution at a time. There is much to do, but we know generally how to go about that. What we don't know how to do, and what no one is positioned to do, from the president down to the lowliest mayor, is to revamp the universe of public institutions as a whole to achieve not only cost-effectiveness but better outcomes as well.

While it is economically imperative to attend to the costs of the public sector, there is an additional, much more important reason, which is that it is morally imperative to do so. Because the institutions of government are essential, paying for them is obligatory. This creates a moral obligation on the part of government to do what it has been directed to do satisfactorily and at reasonable cost.

In the course of thinking about these matters we must also take note of Francis Fukuyama's admonition in his monumental *The Origins of Political Order*: "In the developed world, we take the existence of government so much for granted that we sometimes forget how difficult it was to create."[3] Creating decent government has, in fact, proven to be difficult in the extreme. S.E. Finer's three-volume *The History of Government* tells the story of polities around the world from their earliest forms to the beginning of the twentieth century. Astoundingly few of them contributed to the well-being of their people.[4] In historic terms the performance of our country's government—including federal, state, and local institutions—has been exemplary for over 200 years. These institutions are profoundly valuable.

Endnotes

1 And this is so when things are normal. Add natural and man-made disasters to the picture, and the need for government becomes even more urgent. The virtual absence of government in post-hurricane Haiti was the most fundamental impediment to the extension of short-term aid and preparation for long-term recovery. Government's shortcomings in post-hurricane New Orleans have been extensively chronicled. Consider the situation in post-earthquake and tsunami Japan.

2 Tyler Cowen, *The Great Stagnation* (New York: Dutton, 2011), Kindle edition, Section 262-275.

3 Francis Fukuyama, *The Origins of Political Order* (New York: Farrar, Straus & Giroux, 2011), Kindle edition, Chapter 1, The Necessity of Politics, "Fantasies of Statelessness."

4 S.E. Finer, *The History of Government* (Oxford, Oxford University Press, 1997), I: 34. At the outset of his work, Finer offers an uncharacteristic and poignant comment in this vein: "It is a commonplace among historians that the peasants in the Western Roman Empire did not rise and fight against the barbarian intruders, because they were so oppressed by taxation that they no longer cared whether they lived under barbarian or Roman rule; indeed, that in many cases the transition was—in the short term—marked by a considerable reduction in taxation, since the huge Roman army no longer had to be maintained. All this is very fine and fair to a historian scribbling away in his comfortable room; but in my view—and it is only a view, of course—if a peasant family in Gaul, or Spain, or northern Italy had been able to foresee the misery and exploitation that was to befall his [*sic*] grandchildren and their grandchildren,

on and on and on for the next 500 years, he [*sic*] would have been singularly spiritless—and witless too—if he [*sic*] had not rushed to the aid of the empire. And even then the kingdoms that did finally emerge after the year 1000 were poverty-stricken dung-heaps compared with Rome. Not till the full Renaissance in the sixteenth century did Europeans begin to think of themselves as in any ways comparable to Rome, and not till the 'Augustan Age' of the eighteenth century did they regard their civilization as its equal."

Political Territory
"Ya Gotta Know the Territory"[1]

While political leadership and direction will be essential if change is to take place, government does not suffer, and has never suffered, from a lack of political input at the top. Government does suffer from a lack of management. If the institutions of government, to which I dedicated my working life and for which I have abiding affection, are to reformulate themselves in recognition of the present economic and moral imperatives to do so, strong and capable management will be essential to the task. In this respect, government comes up short. This book is about the managerial deficiency that characterizes the public sector. I wish this subject could be addressed on its own, separate from the political arena, but for reasons we will consider, the management of government institutions can only be contemplated in a political context.

Public Executives and Managers

To the extent that we think about management in the public sector, which, lamentably, is very little if at all, we think about it all wrong. My goal in what follows is to suggest a better approach. Toward this end, I present a big-picture perspective of the major themes that apply. Unfortunately, this big picture is the best I can do, because there is as yet no conceptual foundation to use in approaching the subject. If and when the subject should ever develop in its own right, there will be ample opportunity to explore minor themes.

First, let me address the meaning of a few terms that will appear throughout. By "public executives" I mean those career government professionals who are responsible for the overall performance of the institutions they serve. For the most part these people are knowledgeable, experienced, seasoned veterans. Most of them, but not all, report directly to elected officials or to the political appointees of elected officials. They are, accordingly, at the intersection of the political authorities at the top of the hierarchy and the career government employees who actually operate the government. The term "managers" refers to those career employees who have management responsibility for given parts of the whole. For the most part these professionals report to other career government people. The term "management" will be used collectively to include both executives and managers, as will words like "administrators."

The majority of career government managers and professionals are dedicated to their particular departments and functions rather than to the organization's overall success. This is true for institutions in general—a relatively small subset of managers is primarily focused on the whole. But the term "executive" does not only apply to those at the top of the organizational hierarchy. As Peter Drucker explains, executives are all "those knowledge workers, managers, or individual professionals who are expected by virtue of their position or knowledge to make decisions in the normal course of their work that have a significant impact on the performance and results of the whole." Drucker adds that these executives "are by no means a majority of knowledge workers…but they are a much larger proportion of the total knowledge work force than any organization chart ever reveals."[2]

A great deal of attention is paid to executives and managers in the private sector. They are held responsible for business successes and failures, because they are the ones who make the most fateful decisions. New books, articles, and academic studies of private sector executives are published every day. There is even a developing literature about the nonprofit sector and how its executives can shape better outcomes around the world. This interest is being fueled by an intense competition for financial contributions among non-governmental organizations. Around the world large foundations offer management advice and assistance to nonprofit agencies, and grant funding only to those they deem to be well-managed.

In contrast, the public sector's career executives and managers are mostly ignored. Their political masters are the only ones who are seen to matter. This is curious, given that the institutions of government constitute a third or so of gross domestic product (GDP). One might think that the public sector's management, separate from the political bosses, would warrant consideration from time to time. But one would be wrong. Perhaps it is simply that the political endeavors of elected officials are so much more interesting. Or perhaps, as I will argue throughout this book, we suffer from a collective inability to distinguish between what is political and what is managerial.

My long experience in the public sector tells me that a great deal of what is said by politicians about career government employees, and by career government employees about politicians, is wrong. That is to say, the larger context in which the comments are made is wrong. These groups think they know each other well, but they would be mostly at a loss to define their respective roles in a consistent or helpful manner. As a result, public executives and managers function in a climate of chronic uncertainty in terms of their roles. They do not enjoy the clear context their private sector counterparts enjoy as they think about and perform their responsibilities.

It would be only a slight exaggeration to say that *there are no managerial perspectives* about government. There are only political perspectives. There is, however, a desperate need for managerial perspectives. Because we are accustomed to seeing government only through political lenses, the pursuit of a useful world view for government executives and managers obliges us to reconsider our notions of both political and managerial responsibilities.

There are millions of career government professionals in the U.S. alone—and they have countless counterparts around the world—whose salient values at work are not political. These values shape outcomes of consequence. For reasons that escape me, we have an irresistible compulsion to approach the subject of government as if elected officials are the only figures of consequence. When businesses succeed brilliantly or fail ignominiously, their chief executives and those who work for them are lauded or blamed, whether or not they deserve it. Similarly, when governments succeed or fail, elected officials are credited or blamed, whether or not they deserve it. Career public sector managers are rarely noted at all.

In addition, as I noted earlier, there is a robust literature for managers of business and other nongovernmental institutions who are in search of keys to success and reasons for failure. Graduate schools of business add scholarly assessments and insights into the performance of business institutions, as well as inquiry into normative theoretical aspects of business management. In short, if one is interested in learning how to manage business institutions, there is an abundance of information to be found.

But where government is concerned, the popular press focuses almost entirely on the political universe. No one, for example, compares successful bureaucracies to dysfunctional ones in search of lessons for career managers. The most one might hope for from the popular press is an exposé of excess or ineptitude. Nor is there an academic counterpart to the role played by graduate schools of business. The academic discipline of public administration is a subset of the larger field of political science. Its practitioners study what happens in the institutions of government, but have little or no interest in the *performance* of those institutions. One might think that schools of public administration would do for government what schools of business do for the private sector, but they do not.

Most business and nonprofit managers are familiar with the academic literature in their fields as well as with the popular press. *The Harvard Business Review* leads the way, but it has hundreds of counterparts. Professors in schools of business are interested in what works—they study performance and outcomes. They develop theories, too, but they are outcome-oriented theories, not intellectual abstractions. One would have to look hard to find a private sector manager unfamiliar with this work.

The absence of a comparable body of performance-oriented material, popular or academic, for government career managers is symptomatic of the difficulty we have understanding public institutions. It is widely assumed that outcomes produced by businesses and nonprofits have something to do with their managements, but no such assumption is made where government is concerned. It is assumed instead that outcomes are about the performance of elected officials. More specifically, outcomes we like are to the credit of elected officials we support and outcomes we don't like are to the discredit of those we oppose.

Let me offer a typical example, this one from an article in *The Economist*. The article criticized, of all things, the public sector's use of management consultants. Surely, if public sector managers are responsible for anything, the performance of management consultants should be one of those things. The magazine commented on widespread, expensive debacles in the public sector's efforts to make more effective use of information technology. Failures in the acquisition and use of information technology on the part of government and its consultants are "dispiriting," *The Economist* said, but "the people who are ultimately responsible for the debacles are not the hired hands but their political masters."[3] Unfortunately, there is nothing particularly noteworthy about this example—it's like thousands of others. This is how we think about government.

As I write this, in 2011, Congress is working on legislation that would establish policies on telecommuting for government employees. If this is not a misuse of politicians' time, I can't imagine what would be. This is a subject for junior-level management. The right answers would vary from agency to agency and department to department. For the Senate and House of Representatives to address such a subject for the entire federal bureaucracy is not only a clear vote of no confidence in government's management, it is an effort in futility. This is only one drop in an ocean of futility, but it illustrates the situation.

In such an environment it is no wonder that very few write or conduct research for the use of government managers. The controlling world view is a simple one:

management is for the private sector; politics is for the public sector. That is pretty much the end of the story insofar as government executives and managers are concerned. But it is an egregiously oversimplified and entirely inadequate perspective. Public executives and managers need and deserve a perspective better suited to the realities of their work.

It seems to me that the right place to start developing such a perspective is to acknowledge that, for government executives and managers, it is axiomatic that managerial values must be subordinate to political values. This explains in part why the subject of managerial values in government is so rarely addressed. But the supremacy of political values does not mean that managerial values cannot be articulated or advocated. Nor does it mean that managerial values can never prevail. It only means that when managerial values are in direct competition with political values, the latter must prevail.

The supremacy of political values over managerial values is not unique. Political values prevail over all other values when the latter enter the political arena. We can say this about broad values, such as economic or scientific values, or about narrow ones, those that attach to particular circumstances. Here is a typical headline: "Tax Cuts May Prove Better for Politicians than for Economy."[4] Analogous headlines and assessments can be found about almost any subject, and serve to reveal the larger theme of the supremacy of political values. We don't discard economic analyses because political values trump those analyses when they come in conflict. We don't discard scientific values when the same thing happens. Why must we discard managerial values just because politics sometimes trumps them?

The fundamental assumption of this book is that

managerial values exist in their own right. It is a critical point, one that is almost universally overlooked. Managerial values exist separate from political values. They are about organizational performance and outcomes, are inwardly focused, and constitute a relatively narrow and confined set of values. On the other hand, political values are expansive and connected to the larger society. Political values do come in conflict with managerial values from time to time, but they are not always, or even mostly, in conflict with them.

The articulation of the concept that managerial values exist in their own right suggests that government executives and managers are, and must be, more than mere technocrats obliged to follow directions. They are, necessarily and inevitably, the embodiment of managerial values. They are about organizational performance, not about political performance. Managerial performance and political performance are two entirely different things, so they not only can be, but must be, defined and evaluated separately.

Moreover, if government career managers are not about organizational performance, then *no one* in government is. Fortunately, the ranks of government include many who are about performance and outcomes. Public executives are about the performance of the whole, and public managers are about the performance of myriad subdivisions of the whole. They spend their careers focused on those things. The political performance of their political masters is a separate matter altogether.

Political rule is a fact of life, but there is nothing about it that necessitates the exclusion of managerial values or the enfeeblement of management. The word management needs to become a part of the public sector vocabulary. The practice of management needs to become a high-profile endeavor. It is a given that political values will not change. Public executives and managers are not, and never have been, in doubt about that. But politics and management are not incompatible, and if we have any interest at all in improving government's future performance we must stop thinking and acting as though they are.

How the Supremacy of Political Values Works

In late 1979 Ed Meese, at the time a senior advisor to President-elect Ronald Reagan, spoke to a group of Bay Area city managers in San Francisco. He told the group that the success of the Reagan Administration would depend, more than anything else, on the appointment of 3,000 "political soulmates" of the President to senior management positions throughout the federal government.[5] One of his many responsibilities was to help place suitable appointees in these positions. Every new president brings that same outlook to the job, as do the governors of the fifty states, mayors in "strong mayor" cities, and others.

This is the way government is run everywhere. It is, no doubt, reflective of human nature as well as political reality. The narrative that accompanies the political appointment process is the same no matter the political views or agendas of appointing authorities: the realization of the elected officeholders' goals depends on the services of politically committed designees. This is altogether fair and reasonable—elections do and should matter.

Outside observers may describe such appointments as Chester A. Newland did in 1987, calling them "high-level spoils."[6] The appointing authorities see it differently. Richard Nathan quotes President Reagan as having said, "Crucial to my strategy for spending control will be the appointment to top government positions of men and women who share my economic philosophy. We will have an administration in which the word from the top isn't lost or hidden in the bureaucracy... [we will bring about] a new structuring of the presidential cabinet that will make cabinet officers the managers of the national administration—not captives of the bureaucracy or special interests they are supposed to direct."[7]

My personal sympathies are in full concert with President Reagan's stated goals in terms of management performance. Moreover, all presidents and governors have goals, as well they should. They all seek to realize them in the same way. But in practice it doesn't work out. The fact of the matter is that neither the structure of political appointments nor the appointees themselves are actually *about* the management of government institutions.

In the real world, political appointees have two salient responsibilities: to insist upon the politically imperative and to prohibit the politically unacceptable. It would be incorrect to say that political appointees are anti-management—they are not. But they do not *practice* management. They may or may not be interested in management. They are about the political values of the elected officials they work for. They are honor-bound to be about those values and cannot substitute other priorities, even managerial ones, at their pleasure.

One might think that the performance of top-level political appointees would warrant attention, from scholars as well as the popular press, even if the performance of career managers doesn't. But there is remarkably little to be found on the subject. The system of political appointments—at the federal level and in the states—is taken for granted. It doesn't even occur to us to ask what values it serves or how well it serves them.

Not surprisingly, the merit of the political appointment system is in the eye of the beholder. Seen through political lenses, the system makes perfect sense. Politicians feel, quite justifiably, that they have little control anyway. Why would they surrender or diminish what is already paltry? This is the view of the Heritage Foundation, as expressed in a 2001 report from Robert Maranto, Ph.D., in support of President George H. Bush's prospective appointment of 3,000 designees to positions in the federal bureaucracy: "The executive branch is where the rubber of policy hits the road of implementation. Political appointees are vital for ensuring that the president's agenda is implemented."[8]

David M. Cohen of the Brookings Institution, on the other hand, argues that, "The 3,000 appointees who head the executive branch are neither politically accountable nor competent managers. Because of excess management layering, multiple loyalties, and personal agendas, appointees often are unresponsive to their department secretaries or to the White House."[9] If Mr. Cohen is correct, the current system doesn't even succeed at producing *political* loyalty and competence, which is the primary thing it is designed to produce.

In terms of managerial substance, it appears that career managers perform at a higher level than political appointees. A Princeton University study concluded that on a 100-point grading scale, career managers performed ten points better than political appointees.[10] But this would hardly be surprising. Political appointees aren't there to score well on such a scale; they would be better evaluated according to their political contributions.

There is even a book for political appointees advising them how to succeed in Washington by working successfully with career government executives and managers.[11] Many might find the tone of this book, which is consistent with the tone employed by both supporters and opponents of the current system, surprising. One might expect the intersection between career government's highest-ranking people and the political appointees they work for to be characterized by suspicion and hostility. Imagine being a political appointee and taking charge of a department or office staffed by career people whose knowledge and experience vastly outweigh your own. Conversely, imagine being a career person who will serve rotating political bosses over the long term. Neither is an easy proposition. What is remarkable and auspicious is that by almost all accounts the interface with career executives and staffers works to the satisfaction of elected officials and their political appointees. Making that interface work is, after all, what career government executives and managers do. The efficaciousness of the whole business is another matter.

It isn't clear if anyone knows how many political appointees there are at the federal level or in state government either. Most reports indicate that the president is responsible for about 3,000 appointments. Many of those appointees make their own appointments, however, so the total is far greater. John Kamensky puts the number of political appointments in the federal government at 6,000; the *Plum Book*, which lists political jobs at the federal level, indicates that there are 8,000 in total, though many of these are part-time.[12] Whatever the actual figure, one thing is for certain: the White House utterly lacks the capacity to supervise the performance of those appointees. They are pretty much on their own unless and until they earn the disapproval of their political superiors.

Political appointees suffer from multiple limitations beyond their control. They report to the political authorities who appointed them, but in practice there are no formal systems of oversight. Every new administration starts from scratch. Success on the part of political appointees is, by definition, political, proportionate to and reflective of success on the part of the political authorities to whom they are responsible. The priorities of political appointees must be the priorities of their political bosses. Those priorities come from above them in the structure. Inevitably the crises of the day must be addressed before the crises of the year, much less the decade. Finally, the tenures of political appointees are the same as the elected officials to whom they are accountable.

The managerial issues facing government institutions exist independent of these limitations. They tend to be long-standing rather than immediate. They tend not to be susceptible to political solutions or guidance. In general, they have little to do with the political crises of the day. They tend to emerge from below, rather than above. Their time frames are altogether different from political time frames.

In other words, political realities and institutional realities are not a match for each other. The priority lists of those who assume political responsibility for government and those of career executives and managers are not at all the same. It is literally true that political appointees and career executives and managers live and work in two different worlds. They have learned to adapt to each other rather well, but that doesn't mean the structure makes any sense. They both have necessary and honorable purposes. They are dependent on each other. It is essential that the two worlds come together, and it will never be smooth or easy. But it could be much better.

The universal preeminence of political values means two things for government executives. First, it establishes the highest principle governing these executives' work, which is this: *when political values come in conflict with other values, political values prevail.* It doesn't matter what the competing values might be at any given time. For purposes of illustration, consider a few current, high-profile competitions. Economic values have risen to the fore around the world, reflective of the economic downturn that has gripped so many developed economies. Scientific values are also prominent, in terms of such issues as global warming and stem cell research. Religious issues are also in play, from the place of Islam in the modern world to abortion. Every time a conflict emerges in the political arena between political values and other sets of values, political values prevail. Until the conflict reaches the political arena, various mixes of values can be obtained, but once the political arena is entered, political values do, and must, prevail.

For public executives, the value competition that matters most is the one between political values on the one hand and managerial values on the other. As we have observed, public executives' bosses are obliged and honor-bound to serve political values as their highest priorities. Public executives are similarly obliged and honor bound to serve managerial values as their highest priority. This value difference is a fundamental, everyday reality for government executives, even if it is unknown to everyone else.

The second basic fact of life established by the preeminence of political values is this*: the members of the political class who are appointed to top positions throughout government prevail over those who are not members of the political class.* Government executives and managers are manifestly not members of the political class; they are career employees who serve successive political administrations. At the highest levels of government, then, political status matters more than organizational rank.

Given these facts of life, how much room, if any, is

there for professional management? To answer this question, we must compare and contrast what politicians are about as opposed to what career administrators are about.

Political Work: The Job Description

You might think that the politician's job is to solve problems, make policies, and apply political philosophies. Almost everything people say and write on the subject of politics confirms it. But very little of that actually happens. Let us consider what politicians actually do and must do.

If there were a job description for the position of politician it would in all likelihood include two requirements: *(1) Must have the ability to speak a) for constituents and b) on behalf of government, and (2) Must respond effectively to, as well as generate, political inputs.* It would say nothing about expertise or experience in any aspect of public policy. It would say nothing about an ability to apply a political philosophy to government affairs. It would say nothing about an ability to oversee the institutions of government. It would not even say anything about the ability to work with people. That these abilities were not included in the job description would not be an oversight. Political work includes these things, but they are not at the core of what a politician does.

First and foremost, politicians speak. That is their job. They speak to the government on behalf of their constituents and they speak to their constituents on behalf of the government. Politicians who speak successfully are elected and returned to office; those who do not are not. I would argue that what politicians say is actually far more important than problem solving, policymaking, or the application of political philosophy. It is easy and fun to deride what politicians say, but what they say is what holds us together or drives us apart. Political speechmaking matters.

Making the necessary pirouette between speaking for constituents and speaking for the government is formidably difficult. Obtaining office almost always requires aspiring candidates to criticize and oppose something about the government. Immediately upon taking office, however, these politicians become part of the government and are obliged to speak on its behalf. The longer one holds office, and the higher the office held, the more one is called upon to do this.

Speaking both for and against the same thing comes naturally to very few people. Most politicians are much better at one or the other of these tasks, and strongly prefer one or the other. Unfortunately for them, political opponents will exploit either deficiency.

Elected officials also have a second pirouette to perform, this one between values and interests. Most elected officials are motivated to enter the political arena by a commitment to certain political values. Their commitment to these values is sincere and admirable. The political arena is about the competition of interests, even if most of what is said about those conflicts is expressed in terms of political values. Talking about values is much more palatable than talking about interests. Values are admirable; in comparison, interests are crass. Everyone is more comfortable talking about values, ideology, and principles than talking about raw interests. Successful politicians therefore become expert at speaking of competing interests in terms of competing values.

Almost every politician, even at the local level, is asked to speak to multiple groups every day, and cover a multitude of subjects. Politicians are also obliged to speak to the media on demand. Choreographing these appearances alone is a major undertaking, and few politicians can meet the demands they face in these regards. Moreover, most people need to prepare remarks before delivering them, and politicians are no exception. The time demands associated with speaking are overwhelming. It is inescapable that politicians are, and must be, nearly full-time public speakers. They don't have to be accomplished speakers, but they must speak to their constituents' satisfaction above all other things.

It is of singular importance that when elected officials speak they do so in the first person. Their right to do so has been conferred on them as election winners. They speak for themselves personally as well as for the offices they hold. It is not an accident that when the president delivers the State of the Union speech the first person singular is in constant use. Governors and mayors do the same in their own versions of that speech. Legislators, too, employ the first person singular. Elected officials are the only ones in government who can speak in this manner, so the prerogative to speak in the first person distinguishes them from everyone else in government.

The second part of the job description, responding to and generating political inputs, is in itself a full-time job. Every elected official is on the receiving end of thousands of demands. They come in phone calls, letters, emails, and texts. They come as requests for meetings and appearances. They come from constituents, from potential supporters or opponents, from interest groups, and from other politicians. Each one of these demands is a political input and contributes to the political landscape. Political forces engage in continuous, never-ending, never-suspended quests to obtain advantage and prevent disadvantage. Politicians receive political inputs much like 9-1-1 dispatchers receive emergency calls. Indeed, a typical day for a politician is more like one for a busy emergency dispatcher than any other job I can think of. Because only those political inputs with the highest profiles come to the attention of outsiders, the urgency and intensity of this aspect of the politician's job is known only to insiders. Every day politicians face an onslaught of demands to which they must respond. Failing to respond is not an option.

There is precious little time for politicians to develop inputs of their own, though that is an important goal. Politicians do not arrive on the scene with blank slates waiting for them. They work under remorseless and ceaseless scrutiny and pressure. Maneuvering room is far harder to come by than outsiders imagine. The more successful and senior politicians become, the greater the chance of advancing their own inputs, as opposed to those of supporters, and the better the odds of surviving those periodic instances in which they are unwilling to advance their supporters' causes and interests.

Receiving political inputs is an obligatory burden. The opportunity to initiate them is what politicians cherish above all other things. Most politicians are legislators, and make their inputs in shaping legislation. Politicians in executive roles have a different focus, shaping the performance of government institutions by exercising the powers that go with each position. But legislative and executive politicians are intricately dependent on each other, and can and do deliver both good and bad news to each other. The sum of political inputs made by elected officials is a dizzying proposition on any given day, much less in total over time.

Every day politicians advance some agendas and retard others. Successful politicians must produce outcomes satisfactory to their supporters in both regards. They must lend their energies and attach their names to things that produce advantage, and disassociate themselves from things that produce disadvantage. This is where raw political skills come into play; it is one thing to say what one wants to accomplish or prevent, but another to actually accomplish it.

Politicians as Sole Practitioners

Elected officials are sole practitioners. They do not join teams, partnerships, firms, or companies. There are no organization charts for them to fit into, and no organizational support systems they can turn to. Politicians succeed or fail one at a time. Elected officials are not the only ones in the larger political class, but they stand alone at the top of that class. This means they have precious few "teammates," as it were. Elected officials rarely have time to be alone, but their calling is in many respects a lonely proposition.

Politicians do engage in management work. Their first management responsibility has to do with getting elected: they serve as chief executives of their campaigns for office. They select their advisors and key aides; establish priorities; accept, modify, or reject the advice they receive; and in general oversee the establishment and operation of those campaigns. The examples they set as they perform this managerial work inform their subordinates about their values and priorities, and reinforce or fail to reinforce their messages. And such campaigns are difficult endeavors, seeking—as they do—to combine the candidate's message, appearance, advertising, endorsements, and a host of other ingredients into winning formulas.

Most important, every campaign is ultimately about just one person—the candidate. It is not a team sport. Running for office is always an individually burdensome proposition. It is dangerous and tricky to delegate campaign responsibilities to others, because each and every mistake has the potential to bring defeat. Politicians by nature must be tough, resilient, and self-reliant—much about the job invokes the celebrated loneliness of the CEO. But politicians must also fill their calendars with endless meetings and appearances, and manifest empathy morning, noon, and night. It is a grueling combination.

And then, having won their campaigns, politicians are faced with managing their new offices, which means having to shift their focus from getting elected to performing the tasks of holding office. Providing services to constituents becomes their primary concern, because constituents are the ones who put them in office, but that is only the beginning. Elected officials must also manage their relationships with the myriad interests that compete in the political arena, other elected officials, and their own appointees. They must figure out the labyrinths of the legislative and executive processes. They must set priorities and strategies on a continuous basis. And they must constantly attend to the next election, which means fundraising and self-promotion.

So while politicians are about management, they are not about the management of government institutions. They are about the management of their campaigns and their offices. This is quite enough management responsibility for anyone, even the most accomplished managers. In fact, when we contemplate the burdens that come with the territory, it is clear that politicians have very little time for dealing with the institutions of government. Even for those politicians who have a particular interest in them, and many do, dealing with those institutions is at best a part-time proposition, squeezed in as time permits. Even the president and state governors are obliged to dedicate most of their time to the political tasks of their offices.

As a result, elected officials have no alternative but to

turn to their staffs and appointees to deal with the executive responsibilities inherent in the offices they hold. In theory, elected officials and their appointees, collectively, constitute government's top management. In practice, however, these figures are burdened with two high-level, full-time jobs, the first to produce political results and the second to attend to the management of government institutions. It is a virtually impossible combination, for two reasons. The first reason is that there is insufficient time for anyone to attend to both sets of responsibilities. The second is that most people are well-suited to one or the other set of responsibilities, but few to both.

There is another problem as well. Not even the president of the United States has sufficient staff to meet the top management needs of the federal government. Nor does any governor have sufficient staff to meet the equivalent needs of his or her state. But no president, and no governor, can acknowledge such a thing; it would be tantamount to saying "this job is too big for me."

The Political Class

Despite being sole practitioners, politicians do not toil alone. Elected officials hire staff assistants and a multitude of consultants to assist with every aspect of campaigning for and holding office. All together these people constitute the political class. There is little movement in and out of this political class. People who aspire to careers in government decide early on between those that require political neutrality and those that require political commitment. A very few manage to cross into and out of the political class in the course of their careers, but it is unusual. The vast majority of participants in government are either political actors for their entire careers or complete their careers without so much as setting foot in the political arena.

Elected officials, and elected officials alone, can legitimately speak and act for the people. Even the closest and most-trusted appointees of the nation's politicians can act only in the names of the elected officials who appointed them. They know they can *never* act at their own volition or in their own names. Everything they say and do must be said and done *in the name of the elected official they represent.* Even the president's cabinet secretaries can act only in the name of the president, and they are very careful to make this clear at every opportunity; they have no legitimacy of their own.

Despite their battles against each other, politicians have a remarkable affinity with each other—they are all veterans and winners of the election process. This sets them apart from everyone else, even the other members of the political class who work for them. It sets them even further apart from career government employees. In fact, presidents of the United States have more in common with small town mayors than with the highest-ranking career officials of the federal government.

Anyone who has attended a political gathering of any sort can attest to the cohesion of the political class. There are hundreds of events every year that attract members of the political class, along with career government professionals and others who are not part of the political class. At each of these gatherings, attendees separate themselves quite naturally into their separate classes, and there is little intermingling. There will be programs for the political class and other programs for the rest. There is nothing too surprising about this.

Politicians are at home in the political class—it is where they belong, where they do their work, and where they succeed or fail. Those who work for politicians are equally at home in the political class. Career government officials, in contrast, are at home inside the institutions of government. That is where they do their work, and where they succeed or fail. They are not part of the political class in any way, shape, or form.

As a former local government executive, I find city halls instantly familiar. Though I never worked for a state or the federal government, I would be comfortable in those settings too, especially if I were called upon to deal with the kinds of administrative problems with which I have experience. On the other hand, I would be wholly unprepared to join a politician's staff. Despite my years in government, I would be a rank beginner in that kind of situation. I would be uncomfortable, uninformed, and inexperienced, and would have little to contribute. If I wanted to do such a thing—and I have no desire to—I would have to start at the bottom. But career members of the political class would be equally lost if they were to find themselves in career management positions. In those settings they would be uncomfortable, uninformed, and inexperienced, and would also have little to contribute. They would be complete outsiders.

Political Values: The Microcosm

There is one supreme political value. It is not the only political value, but it is the highest one, the one dominant core value. It is the value of holding office. It is shared by every candidate for office and every officeholder, and all other values are subordinate to it. (Who would have thought that all politicians share the same core value?)

As one would expect, there is an abundance of egregious behavior exhibited in pursuit of this goal, from malicious campaigns to the gerrymandering of districts. But the goal itself is noble. It is a manifestation of one of humanity's proudest accomplishments, the creation of representative government. Commentators often point out, in disparaging words and tones, how much time politicians spend raising money, visiting constituents, consulting with wealthy and influential supporters, and deriding actual and potential opponents. But it is necessary for politicians to do these kinds of things. Not to do any of them is to invite defeat at the next election, which is to fail in terms of the highest political value.

When members of Congress leave Washington, D.C., on Thursdays to fly home to their districts, and when state legislators leave their capitols to do the same, they are not leaving their work behind, as is so often said. Rather, they are leaving lesser responsibilities behind to attend to greater responsibilities. This is altogether honorable conduct. Politicians everywhere do their work out and about in their districts and with their key people. Political work is not done in the office; time spent there must be kept to a minimum.

When elected officials change their messages between primary and general elections, when they abandon long-held views for new ones, when they reinvent themselves, they are simply demonstrating their commitment to the value of holding office. It is all well and good for others to say that it would be better to stand for something and lose than to prevaricate and win, but it isn't true. It is self-evidently better to prevaricate and hold office than to stand for something and not hold office.

Senator Judd Gregg of New Hampshire put it this way: "Congress is good at the next election but not good at the next generation."[13] He was right, but we are wrong to think that this is a flaw in the system. The notion that elected officials should be more committed to given policies or philosophical objectives than to election or re-election is inadmissible. To value anything else above holding office would be instantly seen as a fatal weakness in the political arena. Any politician who held such a value would be like a wounded animal in the jungle. That is, any politician who was known to subordinate the value of reelection to any other value, or who even hinted that this might be the case, would very likely not win the next election for that reason alone. Such a politician would wield meager influence and accomplish little. This is the answer to complaints about the performance of elected officials in terms of other, lesser, values than holding office.

The second-highest political value is the value of responsiveness. Politicians must continuously respond to the continuous inflow of demands made of them. The value of responsiveness corresponds to the second part of the job description, *"must respond effectively to, as well as generate, political inputs."* Over the course of their political careers long-term politicians build impressive resumes demonstrating responsiveness. No politician can afford to be "unresponsive." That is why their schedules are so brutal. Political work is, then, at its essence, about two things: speaking and responding. An unresponsive politician is a soon-to-be former politician. An appearance of unresponsiveness is all it takes. This is why politicians respond so quickly to events: they dare not be silent or even take time to consider how best to respond. It is no wonder that first responses are often regrettable.

Political Values: The Macrocosm

Elections happen one at a time, and at the microcosmic level each stands alone. This accounts for the famous saying "all politics is local." The macrocosm, however, is where "the rubber hits the road." The macrocosm is about one thing, and only one thing: who is in power and who is not. This question dominates every aspect of the political arena.

Individual politicians are inescapably part of this vital larger drama. The drama is about answering just one question: shall the current political order be preserved or replaced? It is impossible to be nuanced about this question. It is the core, raw, all-encompassing purpose of politics to answer it, over and over again. Every time the question is asked and answered, the drama takes on a life seemingly of its own. The drama sweeps political actors into a frenzy of activity designed toward one of two ends: the preservation or the replacement of the current political order. This happens at the national level, in every state, and in every region and locality.

We imagine that politicians have great latitude to solve the problems of our time, and we vent our frustrations when they fail to do so. If we reflect on what actually takes place in the political arena, it is readily apparent that not too much in the way of political energy and work is dedicated to such problem solving. If this were really the purpose of politics, political behaviors would be utterly different. The overarching purpose of politics is not about problem solving at all. This is not because politicians are uninterested or incapable of problem solving; that is just not what the political arena is about.

Senator Mitch McConnell attracted considerable attention when he recently articulated this truth for everyone to hear. Looking forward to the presidential election of 2012, he said that his party's highest priority was to replace the current president. He added that the primary purpose of the minority was to become the majority.[14] Many were offended by this, feeling that producing economic recovery should have been the primary purpose, or at the least that the senator should not have been so candid about it. But Mr. McConnell had it exactly right, and everyone in the business of politics knows it full well. We generally prefer to overlook this axiomatic truth. It is more comfortable, perhaps more salutary, to talk about what needs to be done for the people. But the inescapable truth of the matter is that problem solving is for later, after the right people and views have been securely installed. Because there is always another election, problem solving is always for later.

The collective inability of political leaders to solve problems like the federal deficit, or state deficits such as we find in New York and California (and many other states), is much more about political forces and inputs, not to mention the public, than about the substantive difficulty of the problems. California's budget dilemma is a perfect example. Dan Walters, a knowledgeable veteran journalist who has covered California politics for decades, puts it this way: "Raising taxes by $20 billion a year or cutting that much in spending would reallocate who gets to spend what by a relatively tiny amount (given that California's total economic output in 2009 was $1.9 trillion, in a deep recession)—and while it might affect the pocketbooks of individual taxpayers or individual recipients of state funds and services, it wouldn't change the amount of money circulating in the economy."[15] In other words, the state's budget is more a political problem than an economic problem. The federal government's situation is of a bigger scale: it is an economic problem as well as a political one, but it is still more political than economic.

When we succumb to anger about failures to solve one problem or another we forget that today's politicians would pay a fearsome price for addressing the major problems of our time. They would have to be wholly irrational to do so.

If politicians around the country were to take leave of their senses and come together to adopt compromise solutions to the most vexing problems they face, they would not be in office for long. And their successors would undo their work anyway. Politicians can't go around saying this, but they know it full well. If it were the case that solving big problems would bring re-election, those problems would be dealt with in short order. That big problems remain unresolved is powerful evidence that resolving them would not bring re-election. The failure to resolve big problems says nothing about the competence or commitment of elected officials.

Public opinion polls also contribute to our misunderstanding of political performance, in that we tend to think that, if a majority is for something, it ought to be possible for politicians to achieve it. But the political forces that shape political outcomes at all levels of government are not dependent on public opinion. Strong political forces, which are inflexible, potent, and reliable in terms of their views and probable conduct, easily outweigh public opinion, which is in comparison variable and unreliable. Public opinion polls show that people would accept lots of potential solutions to long-term problems (such as resolving the national debt) that are unacceptable to the political forces that dominate the political arena. As difficult as it may be to deal with the public, it is far more difficult for elected officials to deal with the universe of political forces and the immense pressures they bring to bear on everyone who holds elective office. To be fair, I do not think management can solve these high-profile problems either. Management is about more prosaic things. Management can solve many problems, but not fundamental political ones.

Political work is about getting elected in the microcosm and about preserving or replacing the current political order in the macrocosm. Politics is not an intellectual endeavor. It is not about fact-finding or problem solving or planning for the future. Those things factor in from time to time, but only to the extent that they bear on election outcomes. In truth, political work is far more important than solving the problems of our time. Political work is about managing political interests and passions. It holds the country together. So long as those interests and passions are about the next election, they are not about bringing down the government or the society.

The Larger Purpose of Politics

The successful conduct of politics preserves not only political order but social and economic order too. Indeed, social and economic order cannot exist in the absence of political order. The long history of humankind is one of regime change, everywhere and always. Political stability, especially when coupled with relative peace and prosperity, is the exception rather than the rule. Our current problems are a wonderful luxury very few people over the centuries have been fortunate enough to suffer.

We ought not to take civil order for granted. The consequences of removing just local authority for a few hours serve as warning and example. The 1969 police and fire strike in sedate Toronto, Canada, is a classic example. Sixteen hours of mayhem caused observers everywhere to appreciate the fragility of social order. More recently, everyone remembers the fall of the Saddam Hussein government in Iraq in 2004 and the ensuing chaos in Baghdad, even amidst the presence of U.S. military forces. Venerable Athens is another example of how easily the ties that bind can unravel. When our own national government lost the consent of the governed 150 years ago, the resulting Civil

War killed 750,000, according to new research.[16]

The practice of politics is what holds our country, its states, and its communities together. In the absence of politicians and their endeavors, everything comes undone. At any given time in human history, including today, things are undone in hundreds of places around the world. No place is immune from the danger.

As a local government manager, I sat through thousands of public hearings about contentious matters. At the conclusion of each one, some constituents left the room satisfied and others left dissatisfied. In the course of voting on each matter, the elected officials I worked for had to decide what outcomes they would vote for and what they would say to those whose interests they would vote against. The first of these gets all the attention, but the second matters no less.

S.E. Finer calls the larger purpose of politics winning the "voluntary acquiescence" of the people.[17] When it is won, political, social, and economic order can follow. When it is lost, a new order must be forged. The practice of politics appears to be divisive, not unifying, because every political battle produces winners and losers. Winning the "voluntary acquiescence" of the people is arguably an inadvertent outcome of ongoing political conflict.

Machiavelli, surely one of the most astute thinkers about government, thought that the warring factions of the Roman Republic that are usually blamed for the Republic's demise were actually the cause of its success. He put it this way: "To me those who condemn the tumults between the nobles and the Plebs seem to be caviling at the very thing that was the primary cause of Rome's retention of liberty.... And they do not realize that in every republic there are two different descriptions, that of the people and that of the great men, and that all legislation favoring liberty is brought about by their dissension."[18] The political strife that we fear is tearing us apart may actually be what holds us together.

It rarely occurs to us, in our country, how fortunate we are to be able to fret about our unsolved problems even while our free society and the larger political structure endure. We are utterly convinced that if politicians only did better work, things would be better. Such an outlook seems to me altogether wrong.

These Are Not Political Values

It may be instructive, while thinking about political values, to take stock of things we might think are political values but are not. I am not interested here in whether these examples ought to be political values, only whether they actually are. We have an abundance of history and experience to bring to bear on the subject.

First and foremost, representative government itself is not a high-ranking political value. If it were, redistricting would be done with the objective of reflecting the interests of voters to make their choices. Instead, districts are inevitably drawn to benefit those who have the power to draw them.[19] In practice, democracy is as much about politicians choosing their voters as about voters choosing their politicians. Further, if representative government were a political value, there would be common agreement that candidates who get the most votes should win; the electoral college system, among other structures, would have been long since abandoned. The uncontestable fact of the matter is that the controlling political value is to win elections, not to deserve to win them.

Another case in point is the sorry situation of Washington, D.C. If representative government were a political value, the residents of Washington would long since have been granted representation proportionate to their numbers. Is it not shameful that 600,000 citizens of the capital of the foremost democracy in the world have no representation in the federal government? Does this not violate the very essence of American democracy? Of course it does. The notion that the Constitution intended to disenfranchise a major city is absurd. It is altogether fitting that Washington, D.C., license plates bear the motto, "Taxation Without Representation." Washingtonians have a grievance at least equal to that of the participants in the original Boston Tea Party in particular, and to the colonists in general. *The New York Times* put it this way after the latest setback in the district's quest for representation, "Apparently partisan politics, and the district's large number of registered Democrats, trumps principle every time."[20] I would put it a little differently and simply repeat that political values trump competing values, whatever those competing values may be. Even the most basic principles of democracy are subordinate to political values.

Financial responsibility is another value that is not a political one. This is true in Washington, D.C., in the fifty states, and everywhere else. There are times and places where economic circumstances rudely intrude and it becomes politically imperative to respond to them. There are also jurisdictions where the local culture or history has inserted financial values into the political arena. But history makes it abundantly clear that long-term financial responsibility, balanced budgets, and other similar concepts are not in and of themselves political values. If they were, our country would not be where it is today.

Consider New York. Governor Hugh Carey famously saved New York City and New York State from bankruptcy in the mid-1970s.[21] This did not, however, have any effect on the political values of the state. (Interestingly enough, though, the political values of the city were affected.) And Andrew Cuomo, the current governor of New York, is now doing the same thing all over again, just thirty-five years later. It is not a matter of political partisanship: both political parties have overseen long, slow marches to financial disaster. Economic imperatives are insufficient to generate political response; political actions require political imperatives.

Consider that if we actually wanted to avoid deficits, it would be simple enough: we would amend the tax structure so that it would automatically raise sufficient revenues to pay for the spending elected officials voted for. This would not be hard to do. In such a model, elected officials would be responsible for establishing the tax structure, but the tax rates in the structure would correspond to their spending decisions. This would render elected officials immediately responsible for the tax consequences of the spending they voted for. From an economic standpoint it makes no sense at all to treat spending and taxing as two entirely different things, because they are actually the same thing, but this is what we do and what we have always done. Everyone else does it too.

Financial responsibility is not a political value in other countries either. If it were, the budgets of the world's governments would be very different than they are. The plain fact of the matter is that economic values are everywhere subordinate to political values. (To put this notion in perspective, as well as in fairness, it seems only right to observe that financial responsibility is also not a value held by many of the world's banks or corporations, or on Wall Street, or many other places where one would think it would be.)

Nor are scientific values political ones. Whether the

subject is global warming, evolution, the age of the earth, stem cell research, or any other matter, political values invariably trump scientific values. For the most part, scientific values remain outside the political arena. But when they intrude, they find they are no match for political values. At present the political right is more associated with antiscience sentiment than the left, but the right has no monopoly here. Science unacceptable to the left would meet the same resistance.

Perhaps the best way to summarize is to say that facts are not political values. This is not intended as a pejorative comment. It is simply an observation of human behavior. If every elective office were suddenly held by a scientist, there might be a brief period in which the new scientist-politicians would contemplate altering the values landscape, but it wouldn't last long. If they didn't respond to political realities, they would be gone soon enough. The same is true of managerial values. If every elective office were suddenly held by a professional manager intent on promoting managerial values, they too might produce an initial flurry of change, but would revert to political reality soon enough. It is wholly naïve to think that politicians could, if they only would, change the underlying political values that animate the political arena.

At any given time the universe of political values simply reflects the political forces and notions in play. Political values are not philosophical or inquiring or principled. For better *and* worse, they are reflections of the public and the voters. In democracies, when active and controlling political values cease to reflect the voters, new political values come along and take their place.

I often wondered, over the years, for the sake of my own edification at work, what the Santa Cruz public thought about various things. I discovered two reliable ways to arrive at plausible answers. The first was to commission a professional poll, which the city council often did. The polls conducted were wonderfully indicative of public sentiment as well as predictive of electoral outcomes. (It is popular to disparage deference to polls, but I think more deference would be better.) The second way for me to learn about public opinion was to ask my bosses, the seven members of the city council. Elected officials, as a whole, are more in touch with the people than any other set of individuals could be. When I doubted them I was proven wrong again and again.

I have often thought that there must be better ways to capitalize on the inspired genius that elected officials have to offer in terms of their connection to the public. But I don't know what they are. I do know that there is something profoundly arrogant about someone who has never sought or held elective office to presume to tell elected officials what the people or the voters *really* want. This is a subject on which elected officials are truly expert. The nobility of our politics lies in this connection. This is what politics is actually about, and elected officials succeed brilliantly in this regard. When we find grievous fault with our elected officials, we are only faulting ourselves. They know us much better than we know ourselves. Maybe that is why they sometimes make us so angry.

Politicians as Policymakers

Politicians are often referred to as "policymakers," but doing so is highly misleading. It suggests individuals who make deliberate, intellectual assessments of problems and develop responses reflective of those assessments. It is reasonable to think that the practice of politics could be broad enough to include such an erudite aspect. Anyone who reads editorial pages or watches Sunday morning talk shows would surely think so.

Policy advice is in ample supply. It can be found in every editorial and political commentary. Faculty and students at graduate schools of public policy study the outcomes of government programs and produce scholarly assessments. Think tanks, which are usually associated with a given political point of view, offer a wealth of policy prescriptions. At the federal level, the executive branch relies heavily on the Office of Management and Budget for such advice, while Congress looks to the U.S. Government Accountability Office (GAO). Government agencies themselves do some "policy analysis," but the average person might be surprised at how little of this is actually done "in-house."

Policy analyses rarely serve as foundations for political action, even though it is often supposed that they do. For example, this comment appeared in the January 22, 2011 issue of *The Economist*: "The brainy toilers at think-tanks in Washington, D.C....wield immense influence over public policy."[22] In point of fact, they don't. They serve instead as ammunition for one agenda or another. One can find "policy" support for any proposition one wants to advance. This is why not much in the way of policy analysis comes out of government institutions themselves. To engage in it would come too close to political argument, and the institutions of government must avoid, as much as possible, propositions with political implications. Moreover, were policymaking to take place, it would be utterly unlike political activity. It would be thoughtful, quiet, and modest. It would be evidentiary. It would not identify with one set of political interests or another. Nor would it identify with political ideology.

Consider the agencies of national defense, over which

governing authorities exercise more control than they have in any other area. If there is policy anywhere, it should be here. One could easily assemble a vast array of learned viewpoints and alternative approaches—the stuff of policy—bearing on this subject. David Ormand's *Securing the State* is a particularly engrossing discussion of normative and intellectual insights juxtaposed against actual conduct in the real world.[23] If governments produced policies about national security, they would be based on discussions like this one. But it doesn't happen. And it's not because the government officials who act in this arena lack the intellectual wherewithal to weigh the issues set forth by Mr. Ormand—they have it in abundance—but because it isn't the way things actually work.

In fact, it is not possible for things to work that way. Imagine what a "policymaking political process" would look like. It would be immediately overwhelming, primarily because at any given time politicians confront hundreds of issues. It is easy to dress a few of them in policy clothes, but it would be forbiddingly difficult to attach even a policy sentence to the thousands of pages of political products produced every day. If political work were about policymaking, the political arena would be entirely different than it is. Politics would be about intellectually rigorous assessments of problems together with alternative responses. It would be expert-oriented and empirical. Politicians would weigh complex pros and cons. They would study what others around the world have done to address similar problems, to see what has worked and what hasn't. One can, of course, find such information, but the political arena is not the place.

Even if a solid majority of politicians wanted to make policymaking their top priority, they would be utterly unable to do so. A recent example that provides evidence of this is the response to President Obama's deficit reduction commission. This bipartisan group of political figures produced serious proposals deserving of serious consideration. But they were not considered, because they had elements that were wholly unacceptable to powerful political interests across the political spectrum. Few politicians enjoy the maneuvering room to allow them to even consider proposals like these, much less act on them. It is not the politicians' fault that this is their world. They are quite right to see it this way: they have a choice to make—try to solve the problem and very likely lose office, or push the problem down the road. That is why they choose the latter path.

In order to stay in office, which is and must be their primary goal, politicians make decisions based on political considerations. An excellent example of this is the U.S. Tax Code. We claim that every page of its twenty volumes represents policy decisions, but the truth is that they represent political ones. For example, the code treats debt favorably, so we say that this is to encourage business investment. People are allowed to deduct interest on their mortgages, so we say it is designed to encourage home ownership. People can also deduct charitable giving, so we say it is to encourage gifts to charities. Quite literally, one could go on like this for thousands of pages! In reality, though, every single page of the tax code reflects the rough and tumble of political combat over the past one hundred years.[24] If there is any policy to be found here, it is no more than this: "It is the policy of the federal government to have an income tax."

We should not be surprised by this. When we look back at our history, we consider the Constitutional Convention in Philadelphia in 1787 to be one of our supreme policy accomplishments. And it did produce an astoundingly successful product. But it was much more a reflection of the political issues of the time than it was an intellectual creation of policy. Consider three points, each of which demonstrates the precedence of politics over other considerations.

First, the convention worked in absolute secrecy. If the political forces of the time had known what was transpiring, it is highly improbable that the same product could have been produced; quite possibly, no product could have been produced at all. Here was representative government in its purest form, with just twenty-one political figures taking on the task of representing the universe of political interests. Secrecy was essential to the endeavor. The delegates understood this perfectly, and swore themselves to secrecy; any one of them could have easily sabotaged the endeavor. It is remarkable that no one did.

Second, the political question regarding adoption became a simple yes or no proposition, not the usual extended process of political development. Each state faced a simple choice: to approve or disapprove; there were no other options. This is not the way the political process works except in the most extraordinary circumstances. In fact, there has never been another political process quite like this in human history. As Pauline Maier sets forth in her history, there were actually thirteen separate political processes, one for each of the colonies. Nine approvals were needed for the new Constitution to be approved. [25]

Third, the Constitution was and is still, above all other things, a product of political accommodation. It is also a brilliant, ingenious, and intellectual reflection of Enlightenment political thought.[26] But political accommodations were prerequisites to the formulation of the Constitution's "policies." It was only after resolving the formidable political issues that divided them—meaning for the most part three things: how much power was to be vested in the new federal government, the political balances among big and small states, and slavery—that the framers moved on to setting forth the structure of the new government. Had they not resolved their political differences, or, more accurately, had they not found compromises and language they could all support (they didn't actually resolve their differences), they would never have talked about the more erudite matters that we associate with the Constitution's genesis.

The Constitution meant different things to different framers, and means different things to different people and interests still. This is how political agreements are crafted, with words that have multiple meanings and interpretations.

The Federalist Papers, which are surely among the wisest and most important political treatises of all time, were written after the new Constitution had been completed. They were not the foundation on which it was built; they were the political arguments for approval. This is the way the political process works, and must work. The framers' genius was more in the politics—their product was approved and put into place—than in the policies. If the new constitution had not been approved, it might today be a product of interest to historians and political scientists, but it would certainly not be the premier written constitution in the world.

This is how it works: political products, whatever they are, for better or worse, become policies after, not before, they are adopted. In other words, as is the case with most human behaviors, we act and then afterwards declare, or perhaps rationalize, the reasons for our actions. Over time we have vested the Constitution with high-minded attributes that were not part of the actual historical experience. We have elevated the politics of those documents to policies. It is a fine thing to have done that. But understanding requires us to acknowledge that the policy aspects of the document followed the politics, not the other way around. This does not render the Constitution unworthy of the veneration that has been accorded it; it is indeed worthy. In fact, I would argue that it is even more worthy as a political success than as any other kind of success. I see no need to make it into anything else.

The Constitution is the exception to the rule. Out of literally millions of political products produced over our country's short history, it is one of a choice few that deserves to be called a "policy" achievement. The vast majority of political products are not even close to such a threshold. That is not an insult to politicians, any more than it is an insult to baseball pitchers to observe that perfect games are few and far between. I would argue that we undervalue politics as it is actually practiced and overvalue policy outcomes, especially given how rare they are. We expect much more than can possibly be delivered.

What does this mean for governmental executives and managers? The answer is clear: there are no policy directions. It is therefore an absurdity for career managers to search for policies. If this conclusion seems harsh, consider one last factor. Suppose that every politician is indeed about policymaking, and that my assessment of what actually happens greatly underestimates the policy inputs that come from elected officials. Even if this were so, the myriad combinations of individual policy inputs from thousands of politicians over time would still render political products policy-free for all practical purposes.

The absence of policy direction in an intellectual sense

is a serious problem for career managers. If there were policy directions, management would be on solid ground to make inferences from them. In fact, drawing inferences from general directions is, or at least should be, a fundamental management responsibility. In the real world, decisions and directions in the public sector are all tentative, subject to reversal tomorrow, or perhaps later today. If it were possible to establish policies, they would mightily mitigate against the gridlock associated with the public sector. Policies would provide a context through which career professionals could navigate. But the impossibility of devising policies dictates against the establishment of priorities. This serves the political arena well but fails the managerial arena.[27]

It makes no sense to blame politicians for not doing the impossible. Nor does it make sense to ask career managers to search for something that isn't there. This is known to career managers, but it is not something they can say. If policymaking were a politically viable endeavor, there are many ways it could be accomplished despite the ever-changing roster and views of political officeholders. But no such approaches are likely to be proposed, much less undertaken, because policymaking is not a politically viable activity.

Becoming the Government

At first blush it would seem that if there are no policies, we are left only with what we consider the more crass aspects of political activity. But this isn't correct. Politicians actually take on work that is more important, and more burdensome, than policymaking would be even if policymaking were possible.

Politicians *become* the government. They are synonymous with, and indistinguishable from, the government.

The universe of elected officials in the country constitutes the government as a whole. The universe of appointed executives, managers, and governmental employees do not make up the government; they are only means to ends. Elected officials are ends in themselves. Remember, for example, the absurdity of Secretary of State Alexander Haig's claim to be in charge when President Reagan was incapacitated after an assassination attempt. General Haig did hold a high-level position, but he served at the pleasure of his elected superior; he could not presume under any circumstances to authority that is vested only in the country's highest elected official.

Sunday morning talk shows regularly question elected officials about a wide range of serious subjects. They do not choose their interviewees because they are the people with the most expertise on the subjects they want to address. A search for expertise would lead elsewhere. It is a sheer and absolute impossibility for elected officials to be experts about the subjects they address. Talk show hosts choose their guests not for their expertise, but because they speak for the government. In fact, they *are* the government. They are the ones who matter.

This is why people care not only about the views politicians hold but about their character and how they live their lives. The government is bigger than the sum of its parts. It is not just symbolism. Government not only manifests what decisionmakers say and do, but who they are. This is why people want officeholders to reflect not only their political views but their other beliefs as well. This is why it is problematic when officeholders don't measure up in terms of personal character.

If the presidency were just another job, albeit a burdensome one, it would not age its occupants as it does.

Becoming—personifying, if you will—the government of the United States is not just a job; it is an all-consuming proposition. I once attended a lecture by David Gergen, in which he observed that it is impossible for anyone to be the same person after being president as he was before. This is because the president is called upon not just to *act* in the job, but to *become* the job. To a lesser extent this is true for all political positions. Governors become their states, and mayors become their cities. Elected officials everywhere have two different kinds of responsibilities—performing the discrete tasks before them, and performing the role of the job, which is to *be* the government. It is well and good that we are a nation of laws rather than men, as we proudly proclaim. But laws are an abstraction; you cannot talk to them, and they cannot talk to you. Nor do we know exactly what any law means. We are actually a government of the men and women who serve in elective office.

I have been a frequent visitor to Washington, D.C., for many years. I never fail to marvel at the incongruity between the majestic city and its reputation as a center of political monkey business. No one can visit the Capitol and be unimpressed with the nobility of representative government. And yet the political arena is intensely rancorous and abusive. This is the case in every state capitol and city hall. We revere our government and want it to exemplify what is best about our society, even as we savage it. Holding elective office is not for the timid. It is not just a job. That is why elected officials are willing to accept the abuse that comes with their positions. It is immensely satisfying to compete and win election, and it is a spine-tingling event to be sworn into office. A hint of the heady reward experienced by officeholders can be obtained by walking down Pennsylvania Avenue in front of the White House or standing in front of the Capitol.

I have watched the drama of democracy unfold at the local level for over forty years. The first hint of the difficulties to come is unleashed when one declares as a candidate for office. With a few exceptions, each such announcement produces a frenzy of interest and political maneuvering. Candidates are treated as if they have answers to every possible question. To acknowledge ignorance about any issue is unacceptable. That is to say, it is unacceptable for a candidate to be honest about what he knows and what he doesn't know. It is even more unacceptable, if this is possible, for anyone holding office to be candid about such things. Even newly elected politicians are asked the same questions that would be asked of twenty-year veterans. There is no honeymoon. This is because they have become the government. The government cannot be in learning mode, and neither can officeholders.

Instructions Given

Political instructions to career executives and managers come in three categories. The first category is the instructions of the past. These are found in the laws and regulations that constitute the baseline world for government employees. The sum total of such things is, as we have observed, an impressive edifice. Yet they are actually no more than the formal, enduring directions of the past.

The second category is the formal directions of the present, given by elected officeholders and their political appointees to career executives and managers. These directions come (by and large) from the president to the federal government and from governors to state governments. The picture is more varied at the local level, but all formal directions would fall into this category.

The third category is comprised of the informal inputs

of the present. These are provided by elected officials and their designees who are not in a formal position to give binding directions, but who are nevertheless superior to career officials in that they speak for political values. Every politician is obliged to respond to constituents and interests who have a problem with or want something from an agency of government. And every politician seeks to answer those needs to the satisfaction of the constituent or interest by initiating contact with career employees who can provide those answers. These career government officials are obliged to respond to their superiors in the political class about such matters, whether or not there is a direct reporting relationship.

The universe of political contacts between political figures and administrative agencies is extensive. It is both formal and informal. It is the sum total of all the laws and regulations ever adopted and still in place, the directions issued by elected officials and their representatives, and thousands upon thousands of contacts between political and career figures. If it were possible to take the sum total of directions issued to the executive branches of government, federal, state, and local, we would have ourselves a massive collection. But we would be utterly unable to link them to policy choices or the application of political philosophy.

Politics and Administration

Inevitably, as we turn from our brief synopsis of political values and political work to the institutions of government, we must address the tired subject of "politics and administration." A great deal of nonsense has been written about these domains. There are different viewpoints in every field between those who practice and those who study, but government career executives looking for guidance from the academic discipline of public administration find almost no clear thinking at all about the nature of administrative work. Two interrelated conceptions prevent us from focusing on government administration as a discrete subject. The first is the supremacy of political values, which tells us that even if administration were a valid domain of its own it would not matter because it is wholly subordinate. The second is the view that the political domain extends into every nook and cranny of government administration, rendering the two inseparable and indistinguishable. These notions color almost everything written about the administration of government.

The very job descriptions of government executives and managers illustrate the failure to distinguish between political and managerial responsibilities. Public executives and managers are inevitably told that their job is to "implement policy directions," which is a lofty way of telling them to "follow directions." In other words, the executives and managers are mere technocrats, employed for the purpose of navigating through bureaucratic complexities to implement directions. One looks in vain in government's vast store of administrative content for an articulation of larger and longer-term managerial responsibilities. You would never deduce from the job descriptions of government executives and managers that they are, collectively, responsible for managing billions of dollars, property and equipment worth billions of dollars, and the performance of millions of employees. The sad fact of the matter is that the word "management" is itself virtually taboo in the public sector. Where it appears at all, managerial responsibilities are clearly subordinated to the political. It is no wonder that there is little or no contemplation of management as a separate endeavor from politics.

In fact, the academic discipline of public administration as a whole recognizes no meaningful separation between the two. "The goal [of public administration theory] is not to locate the dividing line between politics and administration because no such line exists, nor is it to ascertain how bureaucracies can be made accountable to their democratic masters... Questions of political power are the central focus."[28] The academic discipline of public administration, then, is mostly not about administration at all.

The notion that politics and administration are inseparable is intended to encompass complexity and nuance, but in the end serves only to render the obvious opaque. The difference between politics and administration is in actuality no more than the difference between bosses and subordinates. Nothing is accomplished by the invention of complex notions when such a simple one is manifestly correct. Almost as an aside, scholars excuse themselves by asserting that "a good bit of meddling...goes on by bureaucrats in policy and politicians in administration," which, even if it were true, hardly justifies the consternation of an entire academic discipline.[29]

In fairness, though, my reading of the literature tells me that scholars of public administration are more disinterested in than dismissive of management. They are, after all, political scientists. Moreover, their products are for scholars only; there is no pretense of writing for practitioners. And not surprisingly, there is little interest in their work among managers or aspiring managers who desire to excel in their positions at work.

Public administration scholars and practitioners have not always been estranged. At its origins, and for the first fifty years of the field, "management was at the core of [the academic discipline of] public administration. But at about mid-century [mid-twentieth century, that is], American public administration scholars lost interest in management theory…losing much of the early close connection between theory and practice."[30] At the same time academicians studying economics and business did the opposite, focusing intently on the work done by and the performance of managers in the business sector.

The overall paucity of performance-oriented material available to the practitioner, together with the vapid nature of the little that is offered, conveys, not very subtly, that there is not really much for career executives and managers to do about the performance of government. Scholars do try from time to time to overcome the gulf between themselves and career government managers, but the effort is mostly embarrassing. Here is a typical offering: "The larger issue facing the American political economy as it enters the twenty-first century is the macro issue of functional placement and organizational management."[31] Or this: "The public administrator's task is to take unapologetic leadership in making American public institutions more reflective of the communal values of justice and equity that are our heritage. The factionalized and fractional political system cannot do it."[32]

As the scholars see it, all theories of management and organization are political. The very title of a classic public administration essay tells all: "A Theory of Public Administration Means in Our Time a Theory of Politics Also."[33] For academicians, the practice of administration is about putting into effect values such as efficiency and equity, which they see as an inherently political undertaking. Moreover, they argue that political neutrality is a vain hope in practice. It is only a short step from such observations to the conclusion that the practice of administration must be political.

H. George Frederickson, one of the nation's leading

scholars of public administration and a professor at the University of Kansas' Graduate School of Public Administration, puts it plainly and simply: "There is little doubt that public administration is a form of politics." The acceptance of this proposition requires public administrators to "recognize the political nature and political biases of any standard" they might use "to guide their decisions."[34]

Moving beyond the academy's views of politics and administration, scholars consider questions of duty such as, "To whom are public administrators responsible? To the Constitution and the laws? To the elected legislators or their subordinates? To professional standards and codes of ethics?" One scholar, having lost his bearings altogether, went so far as to offer this answer: "In the democratic context, public administrators are ultimately responsible to the citizens. It is this responsibility that ennobles our work."[35]

But it is absurd, not ennobling, to suggest that public administrators are responsible to the citizens. It is an invitation to insubordination to their bosses. It is also wrong, in both theory and practice, because it is elected officials, and only elected officials, who are responsible to the citizens. (To be absolutely correct about this, elected officials are responsible to the voters rather than the citizens. But for our purposes this distinction is an intellectual abstraction.) In turn, the political appointees of elected officials report to and are responsible to those who appointed them. Again in turn, government career employees are responsible to their bosses. Public administrators are no more responsible to the public than the army's soldiers. Moreover, what would it mean to be "responsible to the citizens"? It would be like having a million priorities, which as a practical matter is exactly the same as having no priorities at all.

It is sad that the academic discipline of public administration is so remote from the real world and that government managers accordingly cannot and do not look to the academy for guidance or insights. It is also sad that organizations representing career executives cannot promote understanding of, much less the value of, management. It is easier to excuse them than to excuse the scholars, because advocating managerial values inside government would be seen as challenging political supremacy. It would render any advocacy group politically suspect in a heartbeat. There would be no advantage to doing so, and huge disadvantages.

If any organization were going to be aggressive on behalf of managerial values, it would surely be the International City/County Management Association (ICMA), which used to represent only city managers but now includes county executives as well. But here is what ICMA has to say about the roles and responsibilities of government executives and managers in its publication, *The Essential Community: Local Government in the Year 2000:* "One of the most striking features of management…is that the prime role of the manager will be that of a broker or negotiator—but not a compromiser. The primacy of this role is emerging unambiguously today. Tomorrow it will be mandatory."[36] What ICMA is saying here is that local political office used to be more about "community service" than "politics," and as a result there is now less room for management than there used to be, which obliges local government managers to help their elected bosses resolve political matters. This is highly dubious. But even if it were so, it has nothing to do with the intrinsic managerial needs of institutions.

The line of reasoning, if it can be called that, goes from bad to worse: "The distinction between 'policy' and 'administration' always has been fuzzy. In fact, the very existence of a clear distinction between the two has been the subject of a hot debate among professionals and scholars for years. There is very little consensus about the point where one ends and the other begins. The distinction will be even fuzzier in the future. Soon, if not already, both elected and administrative officials should concede that they have a shared stake in both policy and administration."[37]

It is interesting that ICMA felt obliged to note in this report that there has been a "hot debate" among professionals and scholars about the nature of politics and administration. This acknowledges that career government managers have never accepted the academic perspective. I have been inquiring of career managers about this since the mid-1970s, and have never found a single one who thought the academic world view made any sense. Career managers understand full well, however, why ICMA and comparable organizations must be tepid about management. To advance the cause of management would be seen as challenging political supremacy and orthodoxy, and would make ICMA subject to political attacks.

The biggest impediment to clear thinking about our subject is simple and elementary: it is the plain fact that any subject *can* become political at any time. While this is true, it does not follow that everything *is* political in nature. Most things are not political most of the time. It might be a surprise to political scientists, but most things about the management of government are not political. If one were to compose a list of the universe of all possible subjects, with things that are political all of the time at the top and things that are hardly ever political at the bottom, the management of government would be nowhere close to the top of the list. This is known to government managers, but apparently to no one else.

In sum, management in the public sector is not

considered a stand-alone subject, but only a subset of the political arena. Raising it as a subject is itself problematic. Doing so dredges up boatloads of side issues that sink the management boat every time. As a result of this type of thinking, any suggestion that managerial values exist or could exist in government as a set of values separate from political values has no currency. If it is true that managerial values are and must be doomed, if there is in fact no place for them in the public sector, then everything that follows in this book is wrong. If this is not the case, however, we will find that there is much to be said about the values and practice of management in the public sector that has not yet been said. The discussion of management in the public sector could then be as robust as it is in the private sector. It is clear that there is no political need for management. The need resides in the institutions of government. After a brief summary, we will change focus to those organizations.

Summary

The point of this discussion so far has been to demonstrate the impossibility of elected officials themselves serving in either of the two possible management capacities found at the top of organizational structures: that of full-time top executives, or that of full-time—or at least highly active and knowledgeable part-time—board members giving directions to management. Neither can be done. There isn't time. Elected officials have other, more pressing, and more important, responsibilities.

Because this book is concerned only with major themes, I have not even noted the differences between elected legislative and elected executive officials, primarily because I consider those differences to represent a minor theme. Despite their positions at the head of executive branches, elected executives must still focus outward toward the people. Both symbolically and in fact, they stand with their backs to the organizations they head and face the people. They do not spend their days inside the institutions they head; they spend their days representing those institutions to the public, and representing the public to the institutions.

Elected executives are, and must be, about the public, just like their counterparts in legislative positions. For all the same reasons, they have no way of meeting the managerial needs of public institutions. They assume and leave office in accordance with the political calendar. Mostly they have little applicable management experience. Their top priorities are and must be political. Even if they were management gurus before taking office, their political responsibilities are inherently separate and distinct.

Politicians and their appointees can provide political directions and assessments, but they are helpless to shape and obtain performance from government bureaucracies. Reality dictates that only career insiders have any chance of achieving success in administering governmental operations.

Endnotes

1 Meredith Willson, "Rock Island" from *The Music Man.*

2 Peter F. Drucker, *The Effective Executive* (New York, HarperCollins Publishers, 2006), 8.

3 Schumpeter, "The Tale of Mr. Jackson," *The Economist,* January 23, 2010, 65.

4 "Business Day," *The New York Times,* September 11, 2010, B1.

5 He later served as attorney general for President Reagan.

6 H. George Frederickson, *Spirit of Public Administration* (San Francisco: Jossey-Bass Publishers, 1997), 64.

7 Ibid.

8 Robert Maranto, "Why the President Should Ignore Calls to Reduce the Number of Political Appointees," Heritage Foundation, www.heritage.org, backgrounder #1413 (accessed February 27, 2001).

9 David M. Cohen, "Amateur Government: When Political Appointees Manage the Federal Bureaucracy," *Journal of Public Administration Research and Theory* 8, no. 4 (1998): 450-497.

10 "Careerists Make Best Managers," *Federal Times,* www.pogoarchives.org (accessed October 10, 2005).

11 Dave Oliver, Jr., *Making It In Washington: An Essential Guide for Political Appointees* (Victoria, BC: Trafford Publishing, 2003).

12 John Kamensky, "Revisiting the Political Appointment

Process, the President's Management Council," http://transition2008.wordpress.com (accessed 2/20/2011); and *The United States Government Policy and Supporting Positions* (Plum Book) (Washington, DC: GPO, 2008).

13 U.S. Senator Judd Gregg, interview by Charlie Rose, February 2, 2010, *The Charlie Rose Show* (PBS).

14 Ezra Klein, "The Senate vs. the Future," www.voices.washingtonpost.com/ezraklein/2011/12/the senate_vs_the future (accessed 7/10/11). According to Klein, senate Republicans had produced a PowerPoint presentation including slides that said, "The purpose of the majority is to pass their agenda" and "the purpose of the minority is to become the majority."

15 Dan Walters, "State's Budget Problems are Political, Not Economic," *Sacramento Bee*, Editorial Page, December 7, 2010.

16 Guy Gugliotta, "New Estimate Raises Civil War Death Toll," *The New York Times*, April 3, 2012, D1.

17 Finer, *History of Government*, 67.

18 Cary Nederman, "Niccolo Machiavelli," *The Stanford Encyclopedia of Philosophy* (Fall 2009 ed.), http://plato.stanford.edu/archives/fall2009/entries/machiavelli (accessed 12/28/2011).

19 There are some exceptions. California voters recently revoked its legislature's district-drawing powers in favor of a commission approach, but there are a few other such examples. Both political parties hate these reforms.

20 "Taxation Without Representation," *The New York*

Times, January 18, 2011, A24.

21   Seymour P. Lachman and Robert Polner, *The Man Who Saved New York: Hugh Carey and the Great Fiscal Crisis of 1975* (Albany: State University of New York Press, 2010).

22   "The Few," *The Economist,* January 22, 2011, 33.

23   David Ormand, *Securing the State* (New York: Columbia University Press, 2010).

24   The federal income tax was made permanent in 1913.

25   Pauline Maier, *Ratification: The People Debate the Constitution* (New York: Simon & Schuster, 2010).

26   Even guillotine-happy post-revolutionary France, still the home of the Enlightenment, outlawed slavery, regarding it as an abomination and an affront to human dignity. No issue more clearly demonstrates the triumph of political values over other values—in this case the values of human liberty so loudly proclaimed by the American rebels—than the preservation of slavery in the U.S. Constitution.

27   Accordingly, the word "policy" has a plain and simple meaning for federal employees: written directions received other than directions found in law.

28   H. George Frederickson and Kevin Smith, *The Public Administration Theory Primer* (Boulder, CO: Westview Press, 2001), 42.

29   Ibid., 18.

30   Ibid., 123.

31   "Exploring the Limits of Privatization," by Ronald

C. Moe, found in *Classics of Public Administration*, edited by Jay M. Shafritz and Albert C. Hyde (Fort Worth, TX: Harcourt Brace College Publishers, 1997), 465.

32   Frederickson, *Spirit of Public Administration*, 220-221.

33   John Gaus, quoted by D. Waldo, "A Theory of Public Administration Means in Our Time a Theory of Politics Also,"in N.B. Lynn and A. Wildavsky (eds.), *Public Administration: The State of the Discipline* (Chatham, NJ: Chatham House, 1990), 168.

34   Frederickson, *Spirit of Public Administration*, 133.

35   Ibid., 128.

36   Lawrence Rutter, *The Essential Community: Local Government in the Year 2000* (Washington, D.C.: International City Management Association, 1980), 126.

37   Ibid., 128.

Managerial Territory

The "federal government" is a singular noun, but it includes about 1,300 distinct organizations within the three branches of government, and has over 2.7 million civilians working for it. The fifty states employ perhaps 5 million people in thousands of separate departments. In addition there are over 50,000 cities and communities, 3,000 counties, and more than 37,000 special districts. There are also more than 13,500 school districts. All together between 22 and 23 million people work for these agencies. There is quite a bit here for professional managers to manage.

The federal government does four big things and a host of smaller ones. The four big things are Social Security, Medicare, defense, and debt service. Payroll represents only 5% of federal expenditures, so the federal government is not employment-intensive, despite the impressive sums spent. State government is about two big things: education, and health and welfare. It is unclear what percentage of state spending is for payroll, but it is more than the federal share and less than the local share. Local government is about education, too, as well as utilities, police and fire, streets and parks, and a host of miscellaneous functions. Local government is by far the most labor-intensive sector of government, as no one has found a way to bring automation to its tasks.

Peter Drucker argued that when an organization grows to somewhere between 300 and 1,000 employees, depending on the complexity of the tasks it undertakes, a "change of phase" must take place. This is the point at which it becomes necessary for a select number of people to dedicate themselves to managerial matters. Drucker conceptualized it this way: insects are held together by hard skin, while more complex animals require skeletons. Similarly, organizations below a given size can function without professional management, but "when a variety of tasks have all to be performed in cooperation…a business needs managers and a management." In other words, management is to organizations as skeletons are to animals. In the absence of management, "things go out of control; plans fail to turn into action; or, worse, different parts of the plans get going at different speeds, different times, and with different objectives and goals, and the favor of the 'boss' becomes more important than performance."[1] This is an entirely apt depiction; it is exactly what happens in government, and everywhere else, in the absence of management.

Almost every agency of government would qualify for professional management applying Drucker's criteria. Many local institutions—especially cities with city managers and special districts with professional chief executives or general managers—do have professional management and structures designed to enable them to manage. For the most part, however, management is scarce in the public sector. Worse, managerial values are even scarcer.

Interestingly, even the profoundly wise Peter Drucker failed to apply his own remedies and wisdom to government. In fact, he more or less despaired when it came to the subject of government performance. Twenty years ago, in *The Age of Discontinuity*, he wrote: "There is mounting evidence that government is big rather than strong; that it is fat and flabby rather than powerful; that it costs a great deal but does not achieve much."[2] Moreover, he lamented that even the strongest political leaders around the world exercise little control over departments of government. He thought that the "growing disparity between apparent power and actual lack of control is perhaps the greatest crisis of government." He rightly wanted elected officials to be effectual in running the agencies for which they bear responsibility. "We are very good at creating administrative agencies," he wrote, but "no sooner are they created than they become ends in themselves."[3] In other words, the point of maximum political control is when the agency is created. Afterwards, from the politician's point of view, it becomes harder and harder for politicians to give political directions that matter.

Drucker suggested two answers to these failings. The first was to "build into government an automatic abandonment process."[4] He wanted government departments and programs to have end dates. The second, he argued, was that government should decide what to do but not do it, that "institutions not be *run* by government but be autonomous."[5] In other words, government should contract out. But in all the years since Drucker first offered these suggestions, the first one has rarely been tried, and the second has met with only mixed success.

There is an answer to shortcomings such as those Drucker identified, however, and it is Drucker's own: the institutions of government require strong and capable management. A revolution in the structure of government is needed. We know that such broad and thoroughgoing change is possible, because the introduction of civil service systems, which transformed government institutions from being wholly political to being strictly nonpartisan, constituted exactly such a change. Even though there has been slippage from the civil service ideals, the institutions of government are still by and large politically neutral and ready to work for the elected officials the public selects.

Exactly what is it that requires management? The answer is every agency and department of government—federal, state, and local. No agency should be exempt. And perhaps even more importantly, we need to find ways to achieve substantially greater coordination and cooperation among public sector agencies.

The most esteemed scholar of the history of government, S.E. Finer, identifies six salient institutional characteristics: "hierarchical; permanently in function; specialized into...various fields; educationally and/or vocationally qualified; paid and full-time; rule-governed."[6] These characteristics produce a strong, professional core in agency after agency, which is a fine and necessary thing. At the same time, however, these characteristics create resistance to directions from above because professional values dominate. Accountants, engineers, doctors, nurses, scientists, and others quite rightly place the professional values of their fields at the top of their hierarchies of values. Program outcomes, on the other hand, must be at the top of the list for managers, and overall outcomes must be at the top for executives. Managers are about selecting, rejecting, compromising, and modifying other values, including but not limited to professional values, that others do not see as subject to modification.

We have seen that elected officials and their political appointees from the political class have no way of meeting the managerial needs of public institutions. Their tenures are too short and their focus too limited. More often than not they have little applicable experience. Moreover, even if they brought with them wholly applicable experience, their political responsibilities are inherently distinct from managerial responsibilities. Reality dictates that only career insiders have any chance of achieving long-term managerial success.[7] Political representatives, in other words, are essential but not sufficient. They can provide political directions, assessments, and access, but they are helpless to shape and obtain performance from government bureaucracies.

Bureaucracy is not new to the human experience. As Finer notes, many of the characteristics he identified "could be found in ancient Egypt and Sumeria, the late Roman Empire, the Byzantine Empire, the Caliphate, and—most notably—in Imperial China."[8] We think of professional management as new, as reflective of the need to manage post-World War II organizations. But the truth is that management is as old as the organizing of human endeavors—it has to be. We just don't know much about the earliest experiences.

It seems fair to say that governments in the modern world cannot be more successful than their bureaucracies. If we want to make government more successful, we must consider the nature of those bureaucracies as well as what we want from them. We know how to consider them from one or another political standpoint. What we don't know how to do is consider them from a managerial standpoint.

The Patronage Heritage

If it were possible—that is, if it were a viable political option—to fully and exclusively staff the organizations of government with the "political soulmates" of elected officials, elected officeholders would do it. The reason it isn't done is that it isn't possible to do so. Let us consider how this came to pass.

The post-American Revolution experience provides a good illustration. In the void left by the rejection of British authority, indigenous political forces shaped replacement government on the local, state, and national level. It was a remarkable experiment, one of a kind in human history, and the country's political leaders were keenly aware of that.

From the outset the new country's political leaders hired family members, friends, and supporters to do what they could not do themselves. Additional people were hired as a last resort. The modern word for it is patronage—"To the victors go the spoils." The Continental Congress famously insisted on appointing the generals of the Continental Army so that high-level appointments would be reflective of political power. The Revolutionary War itself was insufficient to subordinate political values to military values. In fact, the members of Congress delegated the authority to appoint generals to George Washington only when their fear of being captured and hanged by British forces finally superseded their political priorities.

After the Revolution, the country's politicians continued in the same vein. It was quite possible at that time to replace all the government's employees when elected offices changed hands. The country was small, the entities of government were very small, and the tasks were mostly rudimentary. It could be done, so it was done.

The system quickly became one in which all government employees were obliged to contribute a share of their pay to the political campaigns of those who appointed them. This is the "natural" state of things, just another manifestation of the supremacy of political values. Francis Fukuyama puts it this way: "Tribalism…remains a default form of political organization, even after a modern state has been created."[9]

As the new country grew, its government grew too. The organizations of government became more and more complex, and it became impossible as a practical matter to replace the entire government every time a change in political power occurred. To my mind this is best symbolized by the U.S. Post Office, which in the early Republic and well into the nineteenth century offered some of the very best patronage jobs. Eventually, though, the time came when the replacement of every employee of the postal service would have occasioned a huge interruption in mail delivery, which would have been politically unacceptable. Political forces that could agree about almost nothing else were forced to agree that the mail had to be delivered, and that the post office had to have a set of employees whose tenure was independent of elected officials' tenure. The same circumstances applied in agency after agency.

The Civil Service Heritage

A narrative of reform is generally associated with the rise of civil service systems and the professionalization of government bureaucracies. It is true that reformers advocated the replacement of the spoils system with merit-based professionalism. But it is also true that there was little, if any, political support, from anyplace across the political spectrum, for those reforms. At best the reforms met with reluctant political acceptance over a period of time. Had it been possible to avoid reform, politicians would have preserved the spoils system. The introduction of civil service systems was more about institutional realities and the need to provide continuing government services independent of election results than about reform. There was no other way government bureaucracies could function at even minimally acceptable levels.

The introduction of civil service systems also had the effect of removing government's steering wheels and throttles from politicians' hands. Politicians are right to complain that the size, scope, and complexity of contemporary government institutions render them unsusceptible, or at best minimally susceptible, to political rule. Politicians have always been right to make this complaint. Their opposition to civil service systems made perfect sense. It *is* all but impossible for elected officials to direct the bureaucracies of government.

For better and for worse the most salient attributes of modern government institutions are still the attributes of civil service systems. The structures and practices of these systems are found even where there was never a formal civil service. The civil service heritage constitutes the fifth of Finer's characteristics of bureaucracy noted earlier: the attribute of being "rule-governed." It is almost certainly the most dominant of the five characteristics.

Of course, civil service reforms were not universal in our country. Some regimes became more rather than less political, such as the legendary Tammany Hall in New York.

Political machines like Tammany were organized around voter turnout to keep the powers that be in power. Toward that end they provided everything from employment to social welfare systems in return for votes. Ultimately, the excesses of the political machines stood in such contrast to the civil service alternative that they gave way.

While the civil service model is cumbersome, it is also transparent. Corruption and political favoritism are rare. Honesty is the rule. Career civil service employees attend to their work and remain scrupulously nonpartisan. The model proved to be more successful and enduring than its boosters could reasonably have hoped for. Because of this, as much as we love to complain about them, our public institutions are remarkably open and accountable, due in large measure to their civil service heritage. They are not readily manageable. In that respect, there is much to be improved upon.

Public Employee Unions

As challenging as the civil service heritage is for government managers, the advent of labor unions has further strengthened the predominance of rules. Attention is increasingly being directed to the cost impact of collective bargaining in the public sector, but almost no attention is given to the impact of unions in terms of structural rigidity. For most government managers, the impact of the latter is at least as consequential as the former. It is clear that the public sector is moving toward increased structural rigidity.

Even more important, from the management point of view, public sector unions are leading the workers they represent away from the nonpartisanship of the civil service format and back toward patronage. Over the last few decades millions of government employees—federal, state, and local—have chosen through their labor unions to abandon neutrality for partisanship. According to the Center for Responsive Politics, the American Federation of State, County, & Municipal Employees (AFSCME) is second on the list of all-time political donors. AFSCME spent nearly $90 million on the 2010 elections. AFSCME president Gerald McEntree is quoted as saying, "We're spending big. And we're damn happy it's big. And our members are damn happy it's big—it's their money."[10]

An article on the front page of *The Washington Post* in December 2010 said: "Here are two words you don't hear much lately: public servant. More and more, when politicians talk about government employees—whether they are federal, state, or local—it is with the kind of umbrage ordinarily aimed at Wall Street financiers and convenience store bandits." The merits of the umbrage are not the point. The fact that the compensation of public employees has become a prominent political issue can only be bad for the institutions of government. It adds to the burdens of government executives and managers, because the credibility of and public regard for the workforce they manage is key to accomplishing their goals.

I have never known a government executive or manager who is comfortable with the politicization of public employee unions. Executives and managers have an absolute and inviolable duty to be nonpartisan. It is taboo for them to express, or even hint at, any kind of political preference. They are obliged to, and do, serve their political bosses wholeheartedly regardless of their bosses' political views and agendas. Pro-union and anti-union elected officials must receive, and do receive, exactly the same level of support and follow-through from government executives and managers.

But union members can hardly be expected to do the same. Their labor unions, after all, are spending heavily and campaigning aggressively on behalf of some, and in opposition to other, candidates. This places nonpartisan executives and managers in the awkward position of managing and supervising partisan employees.

The institutions of government exist to serve the public as a whole. Surely all employees of government, individually as well as collectively, owe the same allegiance and performance to anti-union elected officials and anti-union citizens that they would provide to pro-union elected officials and citizens. I doubt that even the most aggressive public sector labor union supporters would contend otherwise. This is why politically partisan public employee unions cannot be reconciled with politically nonpartisan government institutions. Politically nonpartisan unions would not pose the dilemma posed by partisan unions. Many public employee unions and associations are for all practical purposes nonpartisan, as they refrain from participating in the electoral process. This is in all probability the only way for public employee unions to remain viable over the long term.

But public employee unions have another impact too, one that has nothing to do with politics. The introduction of labor unions to the public sector workforce in and of itself adds to the need for management. How could it be otherwise? Unions are about the interests of their members, and that is what they are supposed to be about. There is nothing dishonorable or problematic about this. But when unions, on behalf of employees, bring comprehensive, complex, and expensive demands to contract negotiations, management is needed to counter their proposals. Management must ensure that every line of every agreement is compatible with organizational performance. Similarly, when public employers provide more for their employees, they have a right to expect their employees to provide more in return.

It is labor's job to obtain the most favorable compensation, hours, and working conditions it can for its members. It is an honorable job, and I honor it. It is management's job, on the other hand, to remember that institutions of government exist for the purpose of obtaining certain outcomes, not for the purpose of employing people. Management is about obtaining the best possible results given the resources available. That, too, is honorable work.

The caption on the cover of the January 8-14, 2011 edition of *The Economist* reads: "The battle ahead: confronting the public-sector unions." Inside, the introduction of the article reads: "The struggle with public sector unions should be about productivity and parity, not just spending cuts." To which I would add that productivity is the responsibility of government executives and managers, which they would be pleased to assume if only they were granted the requisite authority. Parity, of course, is a matter for elected officials.

We are seeing bitter political confrontations between pro-union and anti-union forces in Wisconsin, Ohio, and elsewhere across the country. As usual, unfortunately, the situation is almost always reduced to simple sound bites. On the political right the sound bites come from anti-union politicians who claim they can reduce costs by repealing collective bargaining. On the left they come from pro-union politicians who promise to reduce costs but support collective bargaining. These views have in common the assumption that the subject is 100% political, and that politicians are therefore the right ones to deal with every aspect, from the appropriation of public funds to the administration of the most picayune contract provisions.

The legal status of public employee collective bargaining and the cost of contracts when bargaining is undertaken are for politicians to decide. No one thinks otherwise. The impact of collective bargaining on productivity (per *The Economist*) is well beyond politicians' reach. The best politicians could ever do in this regard is to give directions to management. Because management is anathema to both sides of this political divide this organizational reality goes unheeded. If the political right thinks it can manage government institutions effectively by eliminating labor unions, it is mistaken. If the political left thinks that the controlling relationship in the ongoing operation of government is between politicians and labor, it too is mistaken. In fact, in terms of organizational performance, the presence of organized labor serves mostly to add to the preexisting need for management.

Obstacles to Performance

Government executives and managers face three mind-numbing obstacles to performance. First they lack the authority they need to achieve their goals. We have seen why this is the case. It is most unlikely that anything will be done about this. Management has to find ways to perform anyway. The second impediment is structural. I have always hated organization charts, but even someone who loved them would be unable to make sense of the government's organizational landscape. The third is the universe of rules and regulations, which, even if the first two matters were small, would constitute a monstrous barrier to the production of outcomes.

If government magically overcame these three handicaps, government executives and managers would be able to focus on performance and outcomes instead of constraints. They would be more focused on accomplishing positives and less on overcoming negatives. They would nevertheless still have a formidable array of problems to confront, just as all managers do. The universal condition of public institutions is, in and of itself, a powerful argument for management strong enough to ease the constraints public agencies face.

Structure

In 1949 the Hoover Commission prepared the most famous, most extensive, and perhaps still the best report on the federal government from the management and structural point of view. It is instructive to see how long the same big picture situation has persisted. Frank Gervasi wrote a wonderfully engaging book about the Commission titled *Big Government: The Meaning and Purpose of the Hoover Commission*. He titled the third chapter "The Executive Chaos." At President Harry Truman's request, former President Herbert Hoover had recruited three hundred of the best brains in the country to study the Executive organization. After sixteen months of study, they concluded that "the United States is paying heavily for a lack of order, a lack of clear lines of authority and responsibility, and a lack of effective organization in the executive branch. [It] is not organized into a workable number of major departments and agencies which the President can effectively direct, but is cut up into a large number of agencies which divide responsibility and which are too great in number for effective direction from the top."[11]

The Hoover Commission had this to say about the exercise of executive authority: "It was a frequent finding of our various task forces that the President and his department heads do not have authority commensurate with the responsibility they must assume. In many instances authority is either lacking or is so diffused that it is almost impossible to hold anyone accountable for a particular program or operation. This tendency is dangerous and can, if extended far enough, lead to irresponsible government."[12]

The Hoover Commission's modest and politically practicable recommendations were by and large adopted with bipartisan political support. They did improve the federal bureaucracy. But they came nowhere close to the "radical reorganization" that the Commission said was actually needed. The real story was that neither the Commission nor anyone else could deal with the "chaos of bureaus and subdivisions responsible on the one hand to executive direction by the President, and accountable on the other hand to Congress for the use of powers and funds granted by law."[13] And that was sixty years ago. The Hoover Commission's assessment of the governmental landscape is still valid. In fact, the deficiencies the Commission sought to remedy are much more extreme today.

As daunting as the labyrinths of administration within the federal government are, the plethora of agencies and departments at the state and local level is even more challenging. Let me cite a few examples from the state and local sectors. Nebraska has ninety-three counties to serve a population of 1.8 million (less than 20,000 per county), while California has fifty-eight counties serving 37 million (638,000 per county). Indiana, with a population of 6.4 million, has 1,000 township boards, compared to California's 478 cities. It is probably unknowable how many agencies and schools there are.

The number and structure of public agencies and departments across the country is reflective of millions of political inputs made over a period of many years. Few, if any, of those inputs had anything to do with managerial considerations. Each individual piece of the picture is perfectly sensible on a stand-alone basis. But the sum total combination makes no sense at all.

The State of California established a "blue-ribbon" California Constitutional Revision Commission to develop a Hoover Commission-style report between 1994 and 1996. It concluded that "the status quo is no longer acceptable" as "the state's governmental system developed in the nineteenth century will not be adequate for the twenty-first century."[14] The Commission pointed out that the state had over 7,000 units of local government overseen by more than 15,000 elected officials. The Commission called the overall structure "confusing and fragmented," and said that "it is hard to accept that services provided through this structure are cost-effective."[15] Unlike the Hoover Commission's report, which did lead to various reforms, no action was taken in response to the California report.

Arnold Schwarzenegger came to the California governor's office in 2003 vowing to "blow up, not rearrange, the boxes of government." He learned to his chagrin that California's governors cannot do any such thing. However much they might like to have the authority necessary to accomplish this, few if any governors do. Political systems are not designed for such actions. If we are serious about changing anything at all about the institutions of government, the bulk of the changes will have to come from management.

In his January 2011 State of the Union address President Obama said that his administration would propose a sweeping reorganization of the federal government with cost-effectiveness and performance in mind. If the past is any guide, it is highly unlikely that anyone will ask for advice from government career executives.

Rules

Peter Drucker liked the term "government of forms," which he meant to be descriptive but not derisive. He knew that government has to account for what it does, and that bureaucracy is required to guard against dishonesty. In Drucker's words, "any government that is not a 'government of forms' degenerates rapidly into a mutual looting society."[16] Celebrated author Thomas Friedman, also a longtime columnist for *The New York Times*, has observed many times over the years that the trait most admired around the world about government in the United States is its honesty. When a law enforcement officer pulls you over you do not pay him $20 and avoid a citation. When the list price of a permit is $100, the actual cost is also $100.

When we talk about the labyrinth of rules that hamstring government management, then, we must not lose sight of the quite wondrous overall success that government has achieved in our country. Rules are an underlying and essential component of that success, as well as a frustrating obstacle to more success. It seems fair to postulate that Americans are intrinsically no more honest, or dishonest, than anyone else. We can and should take pride in the basic honesty that characterizes government at all levels in our country. Rules are not bad in and of themselves. They are only bad when they produce unintended and harmful results. Most individual rules are reasonable enough; it is in combination that they constitute an unworkable edifice that stifles performance.

It is a gross understatement to say that executives and managers face a formidable array of administrative rules and regulations. The three broad categories of political inputs noted above—the formal products of the past as set forth in complex bodies of law, regulations, rules, and policies; the formal directions of the present, received from all branches of government; and the informal pressures received from multiple sources, largely political—represent most, but not all, of the whole. The whole defies boundaries.

To my knowledge no one has ever surveyed career federal and state government executives with the goal of learning how they would describe the obstacles they encounter in obtaining institutional performance. Let me venture an educated guess as to what they would say if asked.[17] They would identify two major sets of obstacles to performance. The first set would include three areas: first, the administrative rules that govern everything that has to do with employees (mostly the province of "human resources" departments); second, the rules that govern what we call procurement at the federal level or purchasing at the state and local level; and third, the various additional offices and departments that must approve anything and everything of consequence. The last of these would include, but not be limited to, agencies such as the Office of Management and Budget at the federal level and a plethora of similar agencies at the state level. In short, it is not nearly enough to assemble a staff of competent and achieving managers inside one's department; one must find and enlist such people in these numerous other departments as well if one wants to accomplish anything.

The second set of obstacles includes the burdens of working for and with elected officials and their appointees. Referring to how many changes in political bosses government executives can handle, one recently retired federal executive told me that she and her colleagues would ask themselves "How many of these do I have in me?" She said that it typically takes one to two years to establish successful relationships.[18] The challenge is the same every time, and it isn't about the substance of the work being undertaken, it is about trust. Every time new political bosses arrive on the scene, even if no change in political party or priorities is involved, career executives must prove anew that they can be trusted. No one knows more about this than city managers, who do this more frequently over the course of their careers than anyone else. My personal experience validates the critical importance of these transitions to the performance of government institutions.

Many times over the years I asked colleagues in state and federal agencies why management couldn't, on its own initiative, fix the problems associated with the first set of obstacles, so often referred to as "red tape." There are hundreds of possible and plausible answers to this question, but there is one underlying reality: longstanding structural relationships and procedural requirements make every managerial initiative, no matter how small it might be, a major endeavor. As another retired federal executive put it, reform is incompatible with the very "nature of the beast." The beast is inherently unreceptive to change, he told me. The beast wants to avoid repeating every problem ever encountered in the past, and therefore has a set of rules designed to avoid each one of them, the sum total result of which is intended to avoid problems but actually precludes solutions instead.[19]

It is inevitable that contemporary government bureaucracies will have complex rules and regulations. This is true for the private sector, too; consider the rules of your bank, your insurance company, or your telephone or internet provider, just for a sampling. I always wanted the organization I worked for to have just one administrative rule: "Be reasonable." But it wouldn't work for a single day, not even for an hour.

Rules and regulations reflect the complexity of human affairs. Individually every rule has its own logic. It is the collection as a whole that bedevils. There are other issues than the rules, and we will address them later, but coping with the administrative structures of government, coupled with the absence of authority to do much about them, is the single most frustrating and difficult task for executives and managers. And this is so before a direction from a political figure of authority is received!

The Advent of Modern Management

The story of the Ford Motor Company may have been "told so many times that it has passed into folklore,"[20] as Peter Drucker said, but it has not been contemplated by anyone in government. The story, for those who do not know it as folklore, is one of success, failure, and rescue. Starting in 1905, Henry Ford famously built the most profitable manufacturing enterprise of his time; by the early 1920s the company had amassed cash reserves of a billion dollars. Yet by 1927 the company was in shambles. It had become a poor third in the market, and thereafter lost money for twenty straight years, until the founder's grandson, Henry Ford II, "ousted his grandfather's cronies in a palace coup" and replaced them with professional management.[21]

But the Ford story is not about management failure; it's about the absence of management. Henry Ford held to a "firm conviction that a business did not need managers and management. All it needed, he believed, was the owner-entrepreneur with his 'helpers.'"[22] Ford stuck to his convictions, and fired or sidelined any "helper" who dared to make a decision or take an action without orders from Ford himself. The lesson to be learned from this, according to Drucker, was not about Ford's personality, or temperament, or even his grasp of the car business. The lesson was that management is grounded in tasks and functions, and that managers are not just the boss's "helpers."

For Drucker, the Ford story, along with the similar stories of Siemens in Germany and Mitsubishi in Japan, proved that management is essential. "The lesson of the Ford story is that managers and management are the specific need of the business enterprise, its specific organ, and its basic structure. We can say dogmatically that enterprise cannot do without managers. One cannot argue that management does the owner's job by delegation. Management is needed not only because the job is too big for any one man to do himself, but because managing an enterprise is something essentially different from managing one's own property."[23]

For our purposes, it is reasonable to paraphrase Drucker and argue: "We can say dogmatically that *institutions* cannot do without managers." In fact, while Drucker's focus was on private enterprise, he recognized that the need for management was inherent in institutions themselves, not just business institutions. He observed that while business uses the word manager, entities such as universities, government agencies, and hospitals typically use the word administrator. The military uses the term commander. It doesn't matter. Whatever it may be called, "management is essential to organized endeavors."[24]

Managers are about the performance of institutions. The performance of an institution and the performance of its management are the same thing. This is not the case for other employees: many subsets of individual and collective performance are independent of overall organizational success. In other words, the overall failure of an organization does not implicate all of its parts, much less all of its individual employees.

For many, managers may be a necessary evil. But if the performance of institutions matters, management is the only possible means of obtaining it. Managers can and do fail, like everyone else. But the institutional world we live in makes them indispensable. The response to failed management must be replacement, not deletion. The response to incapable management must be capable management. The response to weak management must be strong management.

The private sector has led the way in the evolution of management. In no small measure this is because the results of private sector activity are readily measureable. The overall performance of private sector institutions is scrutinized and assessed by investors, journalists, scholars, and others every day. A corollary of this focus on overall performance is that the necessity of management is now well accepted in the private sector. Overall performance is what management is about.

While overall performance matters in the private sector, it does not rank as high elsewhere. The success—or failure—of a business enterprise is obvious. But who is to characterize the overall performance of a school or university, of a hospital or a city, of a state government or, dare we go there, the federal government? What constitutes success in these cases is not so clear. Moreover, such institutions often have long histories that predate modern management. They typically have large, and highly professional, middle ranks, but are weak at the top. Such top management as they do have is an appendage, attached to preexisting structures. The employees of these institutions like the way things are. Management is rarely welcome.

The plain fact of the matter is that institutions do not like to have their performance assessed. It is a threatening proposition. From the point of view of those inside an institution that has never had management, or never had strong management, such assessments not only do no good but have the potential for great harm. It is not surprising that the insertion of managerial values into institutions unaccustomed to them is an agony. Colleagues of mine who served as the first managers of cities with long histories of weak or no management have uniformly said that it is the kind of thing one can do only once in a lifetime.

If we stand back and look through managerial lenses at the landscape of institutions in the modern world, it is clear that the institutions of the public sector as a whole lag behind private sector institutions, and that some types of private institutions—especially universities and hospitals—lag behind the rest of the private sector. No one in the private sector doubts the primacy of overall institutional performance. But elsewhere, it is a hard sell; the case for management is still a losing proposition.

Looking more particularly at government—federal, state, and local—it seems fair to say that these institutions, with the exception of city manager cities and local special districts that have strong management structures, are analogous to the Ford Motor Company under Henry Ford. Those who hold political office there still want their "helpers," but they don't want professional managers. The result is institutions with a deficiency in top management that impairs overall managerial coherence.

Owners, or owner equivalents, are responsible for deciding the purposes organizations pursue. Management accomplishes, or fails to accomplish, those purposes. If the owners' purposes are perverse, management cannot render them otherwise. Managers who cannot abide owners' purposes must resign. It is a grim truth that more than one government has managed genocide better than it managed anything else. It would clearly have been better for humankind if those managers had been as incompetent as they were immoral.

On the other hand, management deserves credit for economic activity that has lifted tens of millions around the world out of poverty, and for myriad other successes. There is no such thing as institutional success without management success. Managers do not—must not—choose organizational purposes, but management is far from a value-free endeavor; it comes with its own values and standards. Those values and standards have everything to do with organizational success.

Let us return to the question at hand: Can the management of public institutions be rendered compatible with political rule? So far the answer is "no." But it would be far better for our country and for the institutions of government if the answer were "yes."

An Exercise in Thinking about Management

For the sake of thinking through the management responsibilities of government career executives, let us postulate an imaginary, extraordinarily rich family that needs to take care of its affairs. After doing so we will return to the prevailing views about managing government institutions and see if we can't modify them.

Our imaginary family owns vast properties and enterprises around the world. There is more to take care of than the family can handle. The family members agree among themselves about very little. They do agree about two things: they like being rich, and they require the assistance of others to manage their affairs. So the family does what people everywhere do in these circumstances: it hires others to do what family members cannot do. It starts by hiring a "chief executive officer" to oversee its affairs. The chief executive in turn hires others, who will report to her, to manage the myriad parts of the family's portfolio. Given the extent of the family's holdings and activities, many people are retained to perform a variety of services and functions.

In addition to the chief executive and those who work for her, our family appoints friends and associates to positions throughout its domain. Those friends and associates have as much clout as the family gives them. These appointees do not work for, and are not subject to the rules of, the chief executive. So there is no ambiguity about who is who. Family members are family members: depending on how they choose to organize themselves for decision-making purposes, some will matter more than others to the chief executive and her subordinates. The friends and associates of the family members are equally distinguishable. They, too, may be more or less important, but no one confuses them with either family members or employees of the chief executive.

The chief executive, and everyone who reports to the chief executive, constitute the *staff*. The widespread and readily understood use of the word staff confirms that, as a matter of everyday operating reality, we readily distinguish between those at the top of the hierarchy who are principals or owners, the owners' friends and associates, and those who are part of the formal organization headed by the chief executive. Only those in this third category are the staff. The family members and their appointee friends are separate and distinct.

The family can organize itself as it chooses and act as it chooses. It can be dictatorial or democratic, fair or unfair, reasonable or unreasonable, caring or not. It can pursue growth and prosperity or let its estates and businesses deteriorate. It can spend lavishly or be parsimonious. It can contribute to charities or not. In brief, the family is free to do what it will until its money runs out.

The family's chief executive officer, management, and professional staff, and those who work in that structure, are separate and distinct from the family and its friends. They are *at work*. They have a solemn obligation to provide professional advice and services to the family and its friends and associates. The family and its friends can be as unprofessional as they like, but the staff has no such freedom. Family members and their friends can wear their pajamas to work if they want to, but the staff must dress professionally.

More particularly, the family's executives are obliged to think through the interests of the family as a whole. The executives will pay particular attention to financial interests, but other interests will pertain too. It will go without saying, as far as the executives are concerned, that they are in service to the family's long-term well-being. That is why they were hired. If the family wants to squander its well-being, that is the family's affair. But the executives and managers must propose only those things that in their judgment will promote the family's long-term health and prosperity. They just might, after all, want to work for another family in the future, and they will surely be held accountable for the advice they offered.

It is inarguable that our family's management and staff have values and duties independent of the family and its friends. The management and staff are of course duty-bound to accomplish what they are told to do, but they are also duty-bound to promote managerial values and professional performance in the operation of the family's vast and disparate affairs. The family's accountants must conform to prevailing accounting practices, and the family's engineers to professional engineering standards. The family's pilots are obliged to fly properly maintained aircraft in accordance with aviation regulations. If the family has a medical staff, it is obliged to provide professional medical advice and care. And so on.

The family is free to reject all the recommendations of its staff. This puts managers and professionals in the same position in the family as they are everywhere else: they don't get to decide what will be done. Owners, or those who are the equivalent of owners, make those decisions. Executives, managers, professionals, and others on the payroll are hired help. The family's values are supreme, whether they are in concert or in conflict with the staff's values. Owners and owner equivalents bear ultimate responsibility for whatever happens.

Elected Officials as Owners

If we look at government organizations in the same way that we looked at our imaginary family's organization, the role of elected officials becomes very clear. Elected officials are the owners of government institutions. The owner concept works in theory and in practice. Owners' values and political values match up nicely. The prerogatives elected officials enjoy in terms of government institutions are analogous to the prerogatives owners enjoy with respect to what they own. And it makes perfect sense, in every way, for government managers to regard elected officials as the owners of the government's institutions.

The analogy seems even more reasonable when we think about owners' two most important values. The first of these is protecting what they own. It is true everywhere that owners protect what they own from all kinds of harm, from theft and damage to loss of value. They defend and advance the legal rights of ownership. They pass ownership to their children and others of their selection. They resist, with all their might, challenges to the rights and privileges of ownership in general, and to their control over the things they own in particular. The second important value is the desire to own more. This desire plays out in business as a desire to make one's enterprise bigger and more successful, and to own additional enterprises. For others it is evident in the simple desire to own more. (Sometimes, of course, ownership isn't such a good idea. But, consistent with the value of ownership, it is common for people to defend ownership even when it is manifestly contrary to their interests to do so.)

But, as we saw in our family example, there is something else that comes with ownership. Owners can be responsible or not. They can take excellent care of what they own or not take care of it at all. They can value things in accordance with personal preferences as opposed to actual value.

The attachment of owners to what they own is no different from the attachment of elected officials to the offices they hold. The desire to own more is analogous to the desire to hold higher office. The prerogative of owners to be good—or bad—custodians of what they own is certainly applicable to elected officials, who make the equivalent of owners' decisions about everything the public owns, from national, state, and local parks to highways, streets, bridges, and everything else. The public owns a vast set of assets. Elected officials serve as the owners, and government career managers follow directions in terms of how those assets are managed.

As the owners of government, it is only natural that elected officials desire to preserve and expand their authority over, and their access to, the institutions of government for which they bear ultimate responsibility. No one wants to give up what they have. This explains, for example, why the post-9/11 reorganization of intelligence agencies reflects the structure of Congressional oversight rather than the structure of the intelligence agencies themselves, which would be the managerial choice.

In an intriguing essay on owners' values, Meir Dan-Cohen reports that owners often value what they own more highly than the items' actual value warrants. In fact, they sometimes "delight in [a] heap of otherwise useless items." Rather than value things in proportion to their real value, they value things just because they own them. He postulates that an added value—he calls it a "proprietary value"—can explain this phenomenon. And this may well apply to the owners of government too. Political prerogatives and oversight structures often make no sense at all, and cannot possibly confer political benefit. Perhaps these practices are valued not because of their actual worth but simply because they are already in place.[25]

When, as a city manager, I began thinking of the elected officials I worked for as owners—instead of as policymakers or advocates of certain political points of view or just as my bosses—my conceptual framework made sense for the first time. And I feel the same way now when I watch the evening news and the Sunday talk shows, or read the morning papers. It makes a whole lot more sense for government career managers to think of elected officials as the owners of government than to think of them in any other way. Elected officials *are* the owners of government. They behave exactly like owners insofar as the institutions of government are concerned; moreover, the impacts of their behaviors on those who work for them fit the owner concept perfectly.

The value differences between owners and managers in our mythical family example manifest themselves perfectly in government too. As owners, elected officials bring and apply their values and priorities to that which they own. They are free to value and prioritize as they will. Professional managers, however, necessarily hold a much narrower set of values, and deal with a different set of problems.

The Longstanding Managerial Deficit

We have a classic "Catch-22" situation. First, it is a given that consequential government decisions are for politicians only. Second, it is a given that the offices politicians hold, including the office of President of the United States, are unsuited in every way to managing the institutions of government. The nature of political work and the elaborately complex structure of government both dictate against it. As a result, the institutions of government have been exempted from the rigors of management. It is no comfort that this is not an intentional outcome; it is the outcome nevertheless. It is an outcome that has been painfully obvious since the 1940s, as evidenced by the Hoover

Commission's report. It is an outcome that has only gotten more and more egregious over the decades. I often put it this way when speaking to various audiences: career administrators are to managing the institutions of government as gymnasts in straitjackets, handcuffs, and leg irons would be to performing their events.

We have our share of political and bureaucratic failures. But the larger landscape of the public sector is actually not replete with them. It is mostly a landscape of politicians performing about as well as it is possible for them to perform, and career government employees doing the same. Nevertheless, the agencies and departments of government suffer from an ongoing structural, institutional void. It is a managerial void. It permeates the public sector from top to bottom. It is both intra-institutional and inter-institutional. This void results from the basic fact that top management decisions are reserved for politicians only. But as we have seen, politicians cannot perform as top management; it is completely impossible. As a result, there is no top management at all.

Peter Drucker challenged top management to "think through the mission of the business."[26] The foremost top management responsibility, he said, is to ask, "What is our business, and what should it be?" We know intuitively, as well as intellectually, that where government is concerned this question is for politicians alone. But as we have seen, the political arena is not a place where such intellectual pursuits are possible. Career managers cannot decide "the mission of the business" in government. On the other hand, if there is no one to press elected officials to decide those things, they are unlikely to be considered or decided at all.

This is what has happened over the decades: such questions have not been addressed.

In the absence of top management there are only disparate parts. Career managers capably oversee the myriad functions of government, but these functions are not brought together into a coherent whole. The result, as noted earlier, is that "things go out of control; plans fail to turn into action; or, worse, different parts of the plans get going at different speeds, different times, and with different objectives and goals...."[27]

It would be a wonderful thing if elected officials could clearly set forth the "mission of the business" for their managers. But there is rarely sufficient political consensus at any given moment, much less over time, to do so. In other words, clear directions cannot obtain enough votes to be approved. In lieu of clear directions, tentative and intentionally vague ones are provided. This is why management is so often left to work without clear direction: there must always be room for interpretation. In turn, this necessity for "wiggle room" in political directions reinforces the need felt by elected executives to place their "political soulmates" in as many places as possible throughout the bureaucracies of government.

Political reality conspires against politicians who desire to fill the top management void. The practice of politics makes it all but impossible. Politicians cannot fill the void themselves, and cannot allow others to fill it.

This leaves government's huge middle ranks pretty much to themselves. There is an abundance of professionalism in the middle. This is, by far, government's strong suit. Even so, few would say that mid-management is robust or even adequate. Most public sector mid-managers pull double-duty: they are expected to manage and also to practice accounting or engineering or whatever their fields are. These professionals confront real and difficult value conflicts in this regard, because their professional values will often dictate one thing and their managerial values another.

I once spent a day touring various private and public sector facilities in our county. My seatmate on the bus was a retired Lockheed executive. He had worked for Lockheed his entire career, and had also served on many local government boards and commissions. He told me that Lockheed did its utmost to avoid combining professional and managerial responsibilities in the same job. For example, the company viewed engineering and management as two different pursuits that did not fit together well. It wasn't fair or advisable, he said, to ask anyone to do both at the same time.

But the public sector routinely asks its professionals to do both. This reflects the public sector's denigration of management in general as well as a budget reality that is more constrained than outside observers often think. The public sector recognizes and appreciates professional values, but it does not recognize or appreciate managerial values. The truth of the matter is that government professionals need management every bit as much as private sector management needs professionals. As Peter Drucker put it:

> The career professional—and particularly the specialist—needs a manager. His major problem is the relation of his area of knowledge and expertise to the performance and results of the entire organization. The career professional therefore has a

major problem of communication. He cannot be effective unless his output becomes the input of other people. But his output is ideas and information. This requires that the users of this output understand what he is trying to say and to do. But, by the nature of his task, he will be tempted to use his own specialized jargon. Indeed, in many cases, this is the only language in which he is fluent. It is the job of the manager to make the specialist realize that he cannot become effective unless he is understood, and he cannot be understood unless he tries to find out the needs, the assumptions, and the limitations of...other people (also, often, specialists in their own areas) within the organization. It is the manager who has to translate the objectives of the organization into the language of the specialist, and the output of the specialist into the language of the intended user. It is the manager, in other words, on whom the specialist depends for the integration of his output into the work of others.[28]

Over and over again, during my years in government, I would appeal to higher authorities in local, state, and federal agencies when something turned out badly from my city's point of view. I would frequently argue that the professional values being applied in a given circumstance were at variance with the higher purposes of the agency, and that the latter should supersede. I almost always found sympathetic listeners. They would tell me that while they agreed with me entirely, they had no authority to intervene. They understood that, from the point of view of the whole, their agency was producing an undesirable outcome. But the top managers I appealed to were not in a position to change anything. My point is not that I was right and others were wrong, but that those in top management positions lack the authority to change outcomes.

The constraints against management extend from top to bottom in public agencies. Multiple constraints line up against every individual managerial initiative. Inordinate effort is required to accomplish anything managerial. Because managers have full portfolios of other responsibilities demanding their immediate attention, and more of them arrive every day, managerial objectives move lower and lower on their priority lists. Most managers do their best to exercise the tidbits of authority they do have. But they do not work in managerially-minded environments. The overall result is that managerial objectives, when they are established at all, are modest and low-impact.

Consider Washington, D.C.'s recent experience with its public schools. A mayor strongly committed to reforming the public school system appointed an aggressive superintendent and vested her with a degree of authority highly unusual for the public sector. The superintendent acted in accordance with the mayor's commitments, and introduced a host of reforms. Then the mayor lost his bid for reelection, the superintendent left her post, and the future of managerial reform was instantly rendered uncertain.

My point about this has nothing to do with the actual job performance of either the mayor or the superintendent, but with the appalling fact that, in the absence of extraordinary political circumstances, management is taboo. Public schools need management regardless of who is mayor. They need management whether or not a high-profile reformer can be found to serve as superintendent and lead the cause. Management ought not to be dependent on unlikely combinations of superintendent and mayor. Every school principal is a manager, and ought to be vested with the authority to manage. So should every supervisor of principals, and so on.

Because we always reduce these things to the attendant political values, the schools issue is being defined in terms of the merits of tenure and teachers' unions. These are important aspects of the situation to be sure. The larger problem, however, is the absence of management. If there is no one inside our schools with the authority to establish and maintain performance and outcomes as the highest values, political remedies will accomplish little over the long term.

In March 2011 newly elected Governor Andrew Cuomo of New York proposed a comprehensive, statewide teacher evaluation system for New York's public schools. On its March 7 editorial page, *The New York Times* was generally supportive, but acknowledged in the course of making suggestions to the legislature that "it will take a Herculean effort to put this system in place."[29] The unspoken, underlying assumption here was that there isn't a school district in New York capable of managing its workforce, and that a statewide political remedy was accordingly required. If it is true that New York's school districts are incapable of managing their workforces, how could a statewide system imposed by the legislature possibly do the trick? Here New York's legislature proposes yet another political solution to a managerial problem.

In April 2011, *The New York Times* reported that New York City schools chancellor Cathleen P. Black had a 17% job approval rating after 100 days on the job, while 23% of adults had never heard of her.[30] I don't know if she was hired for the purpose of managing the school district or obtaining positive public opinion, but I do know that those are two entirely different objectives, each of which would warrant a full-time commitment. A person can work for and with the public or for and within a school system, but no one can do both. The notion that these disparate functions should be combined in one top executive job is absurd.

Public institutions desperately need to be managed independently of who holds political office. If managerial values come and go with every election, or, worse, if they can be in play only when highly sympathetic politicians not only hold office but also succeed in upending, usually temporarily, the constraints against management, public institutions are rendered unmanaged by default. Management needs to be omnipresent rather than being admitted only under extraordinary circumstances.

No one, and no political agenda, can ever again make the institutions of government simple and straightforward and manageable by elected officials and their appointees. Even local government agencies are too complex for that. Many federal and state government agencies and departments rank among the most complex institutions in the world. But the world is abundant in large and complex institutions, and they are not all incoherent and unmanaged. Is the existence of top management in fact incompatible with political rule? Could we not make public sector institutions coherent and manageable without obliging elected officials to do what they would consider abdicating their management responsibilities? That is the challenge.

Managerial Purposes

We have considered what elected officials are, and must be, about. Let us consider the same for career executive and managerial positions. Career executives and managers are, and must be, about two big things. It would be better if they could be about just one, because the more purposes the less time is available for each. In this case, however, there is no help for it.

The first is responding, attending, and reporting to the elected officials who at any given time are serving as the owners of the institutions of government. These elected officials, together with their political appointees, present career executives and managers with things that must be done and also with things that must not be done. As their top priority, government career managers must do, and refrain from doing, as they are directed.

These political imperatives represent a relatively small percentage of the issues before career executives and managers at any given time. Because career executives and managers lack the authority to act on the myriad other items on their lists without the consent of their political bosses, they engage in regular consultations. This is an instructive process for political authorities who otherwise would have no knowledge of or interest in these matters, as well as for career managers, who must think through the potential political consequences of everything they wish to propose. It is also a hugely time-consuming effort.

Working for and with their political bosses, high-level career officials act on the politically imperative directions they receive and consult about other matters that are managerially important but neither mandatory or prohibited from a political point of view. Thus there is a constant flow of information between political and managerial figures. Because of this, when relationships between political authorities and career managers break down, as they do from time to time, government managers are unable to accomplish anything worth doing.

The second big thing career executives and managers are about is organizational performance. Most career managers are more comfortable and more capable when they are focused on their agencies than when they are focused on their political bosses. This is not surprising, since almost all career managers come from those agencies. The performance of government agencies is what they know best. Political performance is not their field.

Career managers face the same problem their private sector counterparts face when they contemplate organizational performance and the results of that performance. Both concepts matter, but while they are related, they are not the same. For better or worse, managers are directly involved in shaping organizational performance but are more witnesses to than causes of external results. Still, it is a given that the purpose of pursuing organizational performance is to accomplish things outside, not inside, organizations.

Given that managerial authority does not extend outside organizations, it is apparent that management is directly about organizational performance but only indirectly about the results of that performance. Sometimes inferior products beat out superior ones. Sometimes people prefer cost-ineffective, or otherwise seemingly undesirable, outcomes. Management must constantly assess real-world results, because they are often confounding. Obtaining organizational performance is the only means available to managers as they pursue external outcomes, but even fine performance does not ensure the desired results. Assessment and reassessment is a perpetual endeavor.

It is curious, given the two big things career government managers are and must be about, that they are generally thought of as being process-driven rather than outcome-oriented. As we have seen, there are good reasons for outside observers to focus on process excess. But process is only part of the picture. My experience tells me that career government managers are an exceptionally outcome-oriented bunch. I have known and worked with a great many people in executive and managerial positions in a host of agencies, and virtually all of them are intensely focused on outcomes. Demands for performance and outcomes are delivered to government executives and managers every day, by elected officials and their appointees, by those with whom agencies interact, and by government employees too.

Government career managers exhibit profound angst about their limited authority compared to their large responsibilities. In fact, this is always the theme when government executives and managers come together. It is one thing when they don't know what to do because the problems they are supposed to solve have no known solutions, or because the directions they have received are convoluted or self-contradictory. It is another, though, when they know exactly what must be done, but are utterly and completely unable to do it because they lack the authority to act.

The Politics of Management Performance

The simplest and most direct way for elected officials to improve the managerial performance of government institutions would be to greatly increase the overall authority granted to career executives and managers. That elected officials don't do so demonstrates that they do not think it is in their political interest. My view is that they are completely wrong about this! Let's consider the proposition.

We have seen that elected officials cannot serve as executives. They have two choices: they can delegate executive responsibilities to their political appointees or to career executives and managers. We can readily compare and contrast these alternate scenarios in terms of political impact, which is the one and only impediment to the second alternative.

For politicians, the downside of delegating to career managers rather than to their own political appointees is that the latter are obliged to focus on the political fortunes of the appointing officials and the former are precluded from focusing on that at all. It certainly sounds like a downside of consequence. But is it, in actual practice? Is it of any real political consequence at all?

Consider, for example, how a political appointee must respond to a sensitive or contentious request or direction compared to how a career executive must respond. The political appointee is obliged to do two things: follow the direction(s) given and follow them in a manner consistent with the political interests of the elected official or officials who gave the directions. The career executive would indeed have a different take on the matter. The executive would be obliged to follow the directions given. But the executive would be precluded from attending to the political ramifications of the directions. The question is, would this be a bad thing for politicians?

The foremost political axiom in play for career executives and managers is this: tomorrow they will work for the political adversaries of the people they work for today. This is not an issue for political appointees: they are accountable to the elected officials who appointed them and to no one else. Career executives and managers, on the other hand, have every expectation that they will be obliged, at some point in the future, to account for what they did and why they did it. This obliges career people to do something political appointees are not obliged to do: create records of directions given and actions taken.

Two questions arise in terms of political interests. The first one relates to the political value of having instructions carried out with political outcomes in mind, as opposed to having them carried out in as nonpartisan a manner as possible. The second one is about the potential political negatives of setting forth a clear record of decisions made and directions given to career government executives and managers. The former concern is clearly short term, and the latter long term.

Political theory has it that elected officials and their political appointees are closer to the people than career staffers. This would suggest to current officeholders that they should maximize the presence of their political appointees. On closer examination, the generalization requires revision: elected officials are closer to their political supporters than any set of appointed officials could be, but they are not necessarily closer to people who do not consider themselves political supporters. In other words, it is arguably the case that, at any given time, the full universe of elected officials is closer to the people than any other group could be. Partisan subsets of the larger universe of elected officials would be close to some parts of the larger public but distant from others. What happens in actual experience is that because career managers know they will someday report to the political adversaries of the people they report to today, they conduct themselves so as to be accountable across the political spectrum. This serves to advance the overall openness of government. The question for political officeholders at any given time is whether such broad accountability constitutes a potential political detriment.

Benjamin C. Nelson studied the "responsiveness" of selected sets of career officials compared to elected officials in 2006. He conducted a survey of fifty-three municipalities as part of his graduate work for a master's degree in public administration. He noted at the outset that academic "conventional wisdom" would hold that governments run by professional managers ("reformed governments using a unity of powers principle," in academic parlance) would be less responsive and democratic than "political/adapted-political cities" (meaning strong mayor cities or the equivalent). Mr. Nelson's research, however, led him to conclude that professionally managed cities performed better than politically managed ones in terms of "aggregate, informational, and engagement citizen participation strategies."[31] In other words, the broad orientation of career professionals who report over the long term to political figures from all parts of the political spectrum leads those career managers to awareness of the public rather than to insulation from it. I suspect that Mr. Nelson's academic advisors were nonplussed by his conclusion.

One can readily see that any danger of powerful, "out of control" managers is fatuous. Career managers, whatever degree of authority might be vested in them, would be checked by the elected officials in office at any given time and also by the prospect of working for the successors of those figures. I cannot conjure up a stronger check and balance than this.

It seems clear that only a short-term political perspective argues for the current system, which combines political appointees with weak career management. It is no surprise that at any given time politicians would prefer to engage with political supporters than with nonpartisan top management, especially if the performance of the institutions of government has little impact on elections, which seems to be the case. Still, a longer-term political perspective would argue for career top management, for two reasons. First, it would improve government's performance, which elected officials could take credit for. Second, it would make for more transparent government, which politicians could also take credit for. The problem with these arguments is that they do not pertain to the next election. The potential loss of the political prerogatives associated with appointing political supporters to executive positions feels risky to elected officials. If something goes wrong, having a political supporter in a key position could be a very handy thing. Why give it up?

In fact, evidence of the discrepancy between short- and long-term perspectives in terms of the role political figures play in management is abundant. Consider a newspaper report of a typical example. This example, which concerns congressional oversight of intelligence agencies, is about the appearance of managing things rather than actually doing so, but the lesson is still clear. The 9/11 Commission recommended a complete overhaul of the multiplicity of elected official committees that purported to oversee those agencies. No one disputed the managerial merits of the commission's recommendations. When it came to implementing them, neither political party was willing to do so when it was in the majority and in control of the oversight committees. Both were perfectly willing when they were in the minority. The headline reads: "Democrats Reject Key 9/11 Panel suggestion, Neither Party Has an Appetite for Overhauling Congressional Oversight of Intelligence." The article goes on to explain that "now Democrats are balking, just as Republicans did before them."[32] In other words, whichever party is in power feels it must be seen to be managing. But whichever party is out of power argues for structural reform.

This is how the short-term interests of current officeholders have always dictated that the current system be preserved. But the longer-term interests of the universe of officeholders are on the other side. The situation is much as it was at the advent of the civil service system, before a fundamental, structural change was recognized as being in the interest of all politicians. It may be that someday elected officials as a whole will come to see the benefits of professional management as they came to see those of the civil service system. Perhaps it would be helpful to designate the current system, in terms of the way politicians perform executive functions, as one of "management patronage." We have moved beyond patronage for rank-and-file employees and professional employees, but not for top management!

Now let us consider the city manager form of government, which is the governmental structure in our country that makes the best use of professional management. We have much to learn from it.

Government's Managerial Anomaly:
The City Manager Form

The first city manager equivalent was hired in Staunton, Virginia, in 1908. City councilmembers had tired of serving on a multitude of committees and decided to hire a general manager to oversee administrative activities. The first formal city manager system was established in 1912, in Sumter, South Carolina.[33] Dayton, Ohio, was the first large city to hire a city manager.[34] Early on, city managers tended to be engineers rather than administrators, reflective of the notion that efficiency was something of an engineering endeavor. Cities are engineering-oriented, being responsible for streets, bridges, sewer and water systems, and the like.

The city manager form came about as the result of two trends. The more important one was simple administrative expedience. It was common for local elected officials to serve in the spirit with which they also joined service clubs (Rotary, Lions, and the like). They did not see themselves as intensely political and were not part of political factions dedicated to longer-term political goals. The local offices they held were generally nonpartisan, and they were happy to delegate administrative authority to professionals because it was not politically problematic. The city manager form of government struck them as an attractive way to govern and operate, and they did not feel they were giving up political prerogatives when they put it in place. The second trend was an outgrowth of reform movements that ousted corrupt political machines. Reformers also saw merit in the city manager form.

Unlike civil service systems, which were deliberately conceived and established, the city manager form of government evolved without a larger vision of what it would become. As a result, the form is more serendipity than intent. Perhaps for that reason, the real significance of the form is overlooked. The significance is twofold. First, it established a modern managerial structure in municipal government. Second, it formally vested organizational performance values, as opposed to political election and reelection values, at the top of the hierarchy.

City manager positions, and those of the career department heads who report to them (police and fire chiefs, directors of public works, utilities, libraries, and so on), are structured to obtain managerial performance. City managers and department heads are not about the political success of the mayors and city councilmembers they work for. City managers and department heads, and others who work for them, are employed for one purpose: to obtain institutional performance. In their own self-interest they focus exclusively on the outcomes produced by the departments and functions they manage. They are obliged to promote the effective and object to the ineffective. They are guardians of the budget; they pay close attention to cost-effectiveness because they compete with each other for scarce funds. In the performance of their work they promote managerial values in government. As a result, these local government managers have a unique perspective; they work in a structure few in government enjoy.[35]

When scholars do take note of the city manager form of government they invariably compare and contrast the form to other forms. This misses the point. The city manager form is not just another alternative. It brings with it an entire set of values—managerial values—that is thwarted in other forms and levels of government. It also brings access to a rich pool of talent and experience—the country's local government managers.

Consider how this works at the local level. When city councils recruit city managers, they evaluate the candidates' managerial performance in their previous jobs. They do not inquire as to the reelection of the councilmembers the candidates worked for. Similarly, when city managers hire department heads they inquire as to their managerial prowess. The city manager form has spawned a substantial pool of local government professionals, all of them performance-oriented and managerially-minded. Once again, it is important to note that these are not just personal attributes, they are attributes required by the jobs themselves.

It is telling that there is almost no movement of executives back and forth between the city manager form and the classic strong mayor form or other political equivalents. People tend to spend their careers in one or the other. Police chiefs, for example, invariably work for city managers in the city manager form of government or for strong mayors in the strong mayor form of government, but rarely go back and forth between the two.

The city manager form of government is now found in about 3,000 cities across the country. City managers often hold graduate degrees in public administration, but their undergraduate educations and their work histories are richly varied. There is an equivalent pool of professionals in every field from finance and human resources to police and fire. There is nothing like this anywhere else in the public sector. But there ought to be.

Nearly one hundred years of experience confirms that the political issues that dominate in city manager cities are no different than those that dominate in other cities. Political competition flourishes entirely independent of city managers. Actual experience with the city manager form proves that politics is *mostly* not about the management of government institutions. If it were, the politics of city manager cities would be different in kind than elsewhere.

The city manager form of government is an historic accident. No one envisioned that the system would evolve as it has. No one proposed to develop a nationwide pool of local government managers. No one said, "If we grant city managers the authority to initiate managerial changes subject to political consent, instead of relying on elected officials to initiate every change, it will work to the betterment of city government." What did happen is that the form of government evolved in such a way as to produce those outcomes.

To my knowledge no one of consequence (I am not of consequence) has ever proposed extending the equivalent of the city manager form to other levels of government. It is a given that there is not going to be a career chief executive of the federal government or of a state government. There are a host of options short of that to insert strong and accountable management to these levels of government. Since no one has suggested any of these things, though, it has not been necessary for anyone to say why they would not be a good idea, which would surely have been said if someone of consequence did urge such a thing! I have had many informal conversations with political figures about the concept, and I always receive the same response, which is that the city manager form is fine for small organizations like cities, but wouldn't work in larger settings. What they mean is that they don't think professional management would work in more politically complex settings.

The unvarnished and irrefutable truth is that the larger the institution, the greater the need for management. There is no such thing—there can be no such thing—as institutions too large for management. The notion that big government is too big to be managed is preposterous on its face. Nor can there be such a thing as institutions too political for management. That is an even more preposterous notion. The federal government, which has the least management, needs it the most. The states, which are by and large as unmanaged as the federal government, need it too. Thousands of other public entities, especially our nation's schools, do also.

Consider the city of San Diego, which jettisoned the city manager form of government in favor of a strong mayor system in 2006, in the aftermath of the public becoming aware of a pension crisis. The crisis was created by the elected officials of San Diego, who cut deals with those who governed the pension system to increase investment return assumptions, which in turn freed up cash in the city's budget, which the elected officials promptly spent to their political advantage. The resulting crisis was created entirely by San Diego's elected officials; it had nothing to do with the city manager or anyone in the city's management. The root of the problem was the supremacy of political values; that is, actions that contributed to election and reelection outranked financial values in terms of long-term fiscal outlook. The lesson that should be learned is that it is management's job, not the job of politicians, to focus on money, both short-term and long-term. When politicians usurp those responsibilities it is hardly management's fault. San Diego's failure was a political failure. Nevertheless, sadly and predictably, the political response to the crisis was to increase political authority in San Diego and curtail managerial authority.[36]

This is why city managers and their associations, from the ICMA to state and local groups, are wary of promoting managerial values. Doing so is invariably seen by elected officials as an effort to infringe on political prerogatives. Raising the subject is more likely to harm than advance the cause, because even in the face of political failures the response is more likely to be the curtailment of management than of politics.

Politicians clearly think, feel, and believe that granting authority to management diminishes, or would diminish, their own. In fact the opposite is true. Strong and capable politicians need strong and capable managers if they want to get anything done. Strong managers would make strong politicians look good, not weak. Strong managers have no desire to intrude into the political arena; they are quite happy to work behind the scenes. They pose no challenge whatsoever to elected officials. The only thing San Diego politicians accomplished by eliminating the city manager form of government was to diminish the place of managerial values in the city institution. It is clear that the politicians involved saw political advantage in this, but in every other way the city of San Diego lost out.

I have abundant personal experience that confirms the compatibility of strong politicians with strong managers. Let me make a general observation, and then give an example. The observation is this: city managers everywhere have a preference for strong and capable political leadership. Weak political leadership is bad for city managers in every way. (If only the political class as a whole could see that weak management is bad for them in the same way!) When the city manager form of government gets swept aside in political turmoil such as occurred in San Diego, it is a sign of political weakness. Strong and capable politicians, like strong and capable people in general, seek the benefits of surrounding themselves with other able souls. Only the weak and incapable are threatened by the strong and capable.

Let me give a specific example. It was my misfortune to be city manager of the City of Santa Cruz on October 17, 1989, the day of the Loma Prieta Earthquake. The earthquake killed 63 and caused $10 billion in property damage, including damage to 27,000 structures, in Northern California.[37] The downtown core of the City of Santa Cruz was destroyed, as unreinforced masonry buildings slammed into each other and collapsed. Three people were killed. Hundreds lost their housing, especially poor, elderly downtown residents. The facilities of companies with a total of two thousand employees were devastated. It was a nightmare scenario. The city government was engaged in emergency response for weeks and in recovery for years.

In situations like that, the roles of elected officials and career employees become crystal clear. The Mayor and the members of the City Council, and only they, could speak for the city, meaning both the people of the city and their government. Mardi Wormhoudt, the mayor at the time, was a vigorous, articulate, and highly capable political leader. She was also a highly partisan figure who was adored by her supporters and feared by her adversaries. In the aftermath of the earthquake, however, she was called upon to speak for the city as a whole, in a manner that set aside politics as usual. She did exactly what Mayor Rudy Giuliani did so brilliantly in New York on, and in the aftermath of, September 11, 2001.

The Mayor and the City Council I worked for were focused on the public and the many emergencies it was facing. As city manager, I was focused on the city organization and its response to those emergencies. These were two different focuses. The elected officials and the city's executives, managers, and employees worked hand in glove, but were never in competition with each other. We knew our roles; we never quarreled about them. We were dependent on each other; poor performance by either the elected officials or the city organization would have extended to the other. If the elected officials had lacked the confidence of the public, or been unresponsive to circumstances, or been rigid or uncaring, or been seen to deviate from their declared purposes, those of us who worked for the city would have been unable to perform. Similarly, if the organization had performed poorly, it would have reflected badly on the elected officials.

If politics and management were the same thing, capable politicians and capable executives would butt heads trying to perform effectively in responding to disasters. Instead, the odds are they will work together better than ever. This is because for a brief time their respective roles are starkly clarified. It is when things get back to normal that things go awry. Perhaps it is analogous to warfare, the classic example where political leaders must decide whether or not to apply military force, but leave actual fighting to the professionals.

The Inadmissibility of Management Recommendations

My observations and experience tell me that what politicians dislike and fear most in terms of management is not substantive performance in the departments of government but the issuance of recommendations based on managerial values. The reports of study shops like the federal government's Office of Management and Budget and the Government Accountability Office, as well as state legislative analysts, are troublesome enough. Politicians are constantly challenged to develop rationales for departing from the conclusions of these and similar offices. Even given the subordinate status of managerial values, there is nothing to be gained, from a political standpoint, by adding recommendations from professional management to the mix.

Further, managerial values have little or no currency with either the press or the public. Politicians have nothing to gain by applying managerial values—it is perfectly reasonable from a political perspective to have no use for them. It is the institutions of government that need management, not politicians or the public or anyone else.

Consider what professional management would, and would not, be recommending. First and foremost, management is about money and about values related to money, such as cost-effectiveness. Individuals who hold the title city manager are typically vested with the responsibility to propose and recommend their cities' annual budgets and to report on their longer-term fiscal health. Management's default position in this regard is to provide elected officials with costs based on the assumption that the city will continue following the political decisions and directions of the past. That is, since management has no authority to amend the directions of its bosses, it is simply advising elected officials of the cost of continuing the status quo.

It is management's responsibility to report not just on next year's costs but also on the long-term costs of the political decisions that are in force. At the local level management routinely does both these things. At the state and federal levels, however, long-term cost consequences are mostly the province of policy and analysis shops. They do excellent work, but they are not responsible for operations, which is a critical limitation. The states and the federal government have abundant opportunities to improve their financial performance; the key to doing this is stronger and better management.

It is true that the most important financial and economic decisions are made at the political level. Management cannot decide how much money to send Social Security or Medicare recipients or schools and universities. But there is an enormous arena of spending below the political level for which management should be responsible. In terms of the age-old onion metaphor, we have an immense onion and only the outer layer is political. Politicians have the prerogative of cutting into the onion whenever and however they like, so they can render this part or that part political at their pleasure. But it is a vast and complicated onion, and it is mightily resistant to interference. As a practical matter, it is mostly beyond political reach. Only insider professionals can effectively and systematically get at the inner layers.

In growing jurisdictions, and in economic good times, management will advise the elected officials they work for of what it takes to maintain service levels to the expanding number of recipients. When managers do this, they are reporting the future cost of past political directions. At the city level, for example, management will figure out how to provide water and sewer, police and fire, streets and bridges, and the like to an expanding population. In economic bad times, management is obliged to propose cutbacks reflective of shrinking tax receipts. Across the country city managers have been recommending steep cuts in city spending, reflective of shrinking tax receipts. City managers recommend alternatives but do not choose them: that is for their bosses to do. Preparing alternatives can raise sensitive subjects such as pension reform.

While city managers have no wish to usurp their bosses' political responsibilities in this or any other regard, they must report on economic reality. When hard choices loom, management must make recommendations. On occasion they can't help but tread on political ground. So long as their recommendations reflect managerial values and not political agendas they are on solid footing. Many city managers have been warning of pension cost problems for decades. They have done this not in a mode of political advocacy but in their capacities as financial advisors. This is a good example, though, of why politicians might prefer not to receive management recommendations at all. Raising issues like the viability of pensions is politically tendentious; some politicians will welcome it and others will want to "do in" the messenger.

Money management is the most basic managerial responsibility. Owners are free to make choices that are not cost-effective, but managers are obliged to make recommendations that are. When told to accomplish something, management must report back with the most cost-effective way of doing it. It is most often the case that the public and its elected representatives prefer choices that are not cost-effective. In fact, my experience tells me that cost-effectiveness is rarely the highest value at issue in the political arena. This is another reason for the unpopularity of management.

As I write this, my own community is struggling over the future of its library system. The application of managerial values to the situation would close the smallest and least-used branches in favor of the larger, better-equipped, and much more heavily patronized facilities. This is the kind of outcome that tests of cost-effectiveness inevitably produce. It is not an outcome that very many people like or appreciate, especially the politicians who represent constituents who would be adversely affected. Nor does the press argue for cost-effectiveness. And the application of the managerial value of cost-effectiveness to public services in general would produce hundreds, perhaps thousands, of comparable situations. It is easy to see why elected officials would prefer not to hear about them.

When we talk about choosing outcomes other than the most cost-effective one, it is easy to become discouraged and think that government is terribly wasteful. But a fundamental fact about government is that by and large it produces excellent bargains. The levying of taxes raises substantial sums and in general produces handsome results, in terms of costs on a per taxpayer basis. Because this is the case, cost-effectiveness is rarely a compelling value on a case-by-case basis. It is almost always reasonable and understandable, one issue at a time, for politicians to choose other than the most cost-effective alternatives. The differences between cost-effective choices and others are often so small as to make the application of cost-effectiveness seem mean-spirited. It is only in the aggregate that one finds benefit in cost-effectiveness. But the aggregate is hardly ever a political issue. Nevertheless, it remains the case that professional managers must propose cost-effectiveness at all times, and let their political bosses accept or not accept their recommendations. This is the most basic of all managerial responsibilities. There can be no such thing as a cost-indifferent manager.

Politically problematic management recommendations are not always about money. They are also about people, including employees, contractors, and others; and about property, plant, and equipment.

Because management is accountable for results produced, effectiveness is necessarily at the top of the managerial value calculus. Cost-effectiveness follows close behind, because there is always another priority to be addressed. Unproductive uses of money; people; and property, plant, and equipment are the scourge of management, obstructing accomplishment. The only difference between the public and private sectors is that in the former elected officials establish purposes and priorities, while in the latter top management performs that function. But the job of producing outcomes through institutions is the same in both environments.

To Initiate

We noted that Governor Schwarzenegger was committed, on assuming office after a recall of the prior governor, to "blowing up," not rearranging, the boxes on the state of California's organization chart. Among other things, he wanted to eliminate redundancies and longstanding practices that, in his administration's view, had lost their utility. He met with no success at all.

I followed the governor's efforts with interest after I happened to read one of his office's reports that identified dozens and dozens of flagrant redundancies that, I would have thought, would have proven easy to address. It turned out that one person's redundancy is another person's essential service. The proposed changes were minor in nature. They were the kinds of things that competent management would have attended to. I remember thinking (wrongly) that they would be of little if any political consequence.

More importantly, I remember thinking that, in the city manager form of government, city managers and department heads routinely make exactly the same kinds of changes on an ongoing basis that the governor was unable to make. Because city managers are responsible for recommending budgets to mayors and city councils, they include changes they think need to be made in their proposed budgets. If the elected officials in charge consent to the changes, they are accomplished. If the elected officials reject them, they are not implemented.

This changes the political calculus in favor of change. At the federal and state levels, and elsewhere in the absence of professional management, even the smallest changes must be initiated and promoted by elected officials. In city manager cities, on the other hand, city managers and department heads routinely restructure services in the interest of managerial performance. These executives and managers must obtain the consent of the elected officials they work for, but there is no need for the elected officials to initiate and promote. If and when political controversies arise, issues move to the political arena for the mayor and city council to decide. Elected city officials give up nothing and gain much in the way of organizational performance.

Politicians are under no illusions about how much managerial control they exercise over the vast estates of government. They know, as Governor Schwarzenegger learned, that they exercise none. They know that it is harder to change something than it was to initiate it in the first place. The government landscape is replete with opportunities that would never make a political hit parade but cannot be taken advantage of without a political impetus. These matters belong in the managerial, not the political, arena.

The authority to initiate change based on managerial values and performance must belong to management. Requiring political champions for every managerial initiative ensures that there aren't very many. The situation needs to be reversed: management's proposals should stand approved unless the politicians in charge reject them, rather than stand rejected unless political figures choose to endorse and advance them.

Anything *Can* Be Political

One of the career manager's dilemmas and burdens, insofar as her political bosses are concerned, is that the latter are free to take on any managerial issues they like at any time. If Congress wants to attend to issues like telecommuting, however ridiculous that may be, it is perfectly free to do so. This is so at every level of government. It is in the nature of the political arena that any subject can find its way there. Every career manager knows and accepts that politicians have permanent passes into the managerial arena. The political arena, on the other hand, is absolutely forbidden to career managers, as it must be. This is not a problem or an issue for career managers. They want nothing to do with the political arena anyway. They have no place there. The term "fish out of water" understates how out of place they would be.

Elected officials, and only elected officials, can establish the purposes of government and decide how much to spend and tax in support of those purposes. Elected officials, and only elected officials, can judge the worthiness of government programs. Elected officials, and only elected officials, can debate these things before the public. Elected officials, and only elected officials, can hold or change government's course. At every level of government, these matters are at issue at all times. They are more than enough to absorb the full talents of elected officials. It is obvious that elected officials are not short of work to do. There is no good reason for them to dedicate themselves to doing what management can and should do.

Management is responsible for operating the institutions of government and accomplishing what they are directed to accomplish. In the private sector, management does the equivalent of the things politicians do in the public sector. This is another reason for the confusion about political and managerial roles. Private sector executives do decide the purposes of the enterprises they run.

The core responsibilities of career government managers are almost never the stuff of political campaigns or political focus. At most, politicians pay lip service to managerial issues from time to time. Given this big picture, politicians and career managers ought to fit together reasonably well. That is why it is so tempting to think that, someday, management will be a given at the state and federal levels, not just the local level.

Think of the subjects covered by presidents in their "State of the Union" speeches. Governors, mayors, and other elected officials routinely present analogous remarks to their constituents. In these addresses they talk about the major issues of the day, the responses they propose, and why their responses should be approved and others not. They do their best to explain how we got where we are and what they propose to do next. These are always big-picture speeches. They are almost always dignified and constructive. Most important for our purposes, they are always about the vital political issues of the day. These are the highest-priority issues elected officials are attending to. Moreover, these speeches are perfect illustrations of elected officials at their best, communicating with the people.

Imagine the counterpart speeches that would be given by career government executives, if they were to do so. (There is no danger of this happening.) They would report on the state of the institutions of government, including recent successes and failures; budgets; employees; property, plant, and equipment; future plans; risks; and opportunities. There would be no overlap between the speeches of the elected officials and the appointed executives. The lack of overlap would not have to be planned; it would simply result from the lack of overlapping focus and responsibilities.

The separateness of politics and management is evident in other ways too. We have noted that politicians speak, but we have not noted that executives and managers write instead, especially when the content might be of public interest. The latter write in part because only politicians can speak to the public. But even more importantly, written records are the essence of their work. Moreover, when executives and managers do speak, which is largely to each other and to those who report to them, they use the plural "we," because they are speaking for an institution and not for themselves personally. When elected officials speak, they do so in the first person singular. They are speaking for themselves personally and also for the government.

The establishment of strong management throughout government would not require delegation on the part of elected officials. All that would be necessary is for elected officials to do their political work as they should and to structure government institutions to enable career executives and managers to perform managerial work. In fact, strong management would render elected officials much more important to the institutions of government than they are in its absence, because it would regularly present the elected "owners" of government with a small number of highly consequential things to be decided. In the absence of management, elected officials make myriad inconsequential decisions, but studiously avoid making consequential ones.

How Not to Reform Government

The exact same reform process is repeated over and over again, on both large and small scales. A problem emerges. It is within the purview of a government department or a collection of departments. It is clear that the department or departments are not structured as needed. Something must be done. Elected officials feel responsible for doing it. Accordingly, and inevitably, they summon and empanel a team of politically respected and experienced hands who recommend what to do. Some portion of what is recommended is accomplished. The matter is not attended to again until the whole process has to be repeated. This happens at the federal level, in every one of the fifty states, and at the local level too. The political need for a response is met. That is the only need that is met; underlying managerial needs are never considered.

Consider for a moment the two most prominent such exercises. The first was the Hoover Commission, which we considered above. The second is the 9/11 Commission, which was created by Congress in 2002 in the aftermath of the terrorist attacks of September 11, 2001. The Commission investigated broadly and made sweeping recommendations about the structure and operations of the federal government's intelligence agencies. In the end eleven federal agencies were consolidated into one agency under a new Director of National Intelligence. The CIA and the FBI were not incorporated into the new agency.

The point I want to make is this. Neither the Hoover Commission nor the 9/11 Commission included a single career federal government executive. The subject of both commissions was how to reorganize government functions and departments. But no one who had ever worked in any of these departments or ever would work in one of these departments was part of the process. The reason is plain and simple: the problems to be addressed were seen as political problems that required political solutions. They were not seen as management problems requiring management solutions.

The Hoover Commission and the 9/11 Commission consisted of estimable, capable, accomplished people who performed splendidly. Their work had political aspects, and they accomplished those aspects successfully. But neither of these commissions was in a position to reorganize the federal government. And no matter who does it, such a thing could never be a one-time proposition. The federal government is a massive place; reorganizing should be an intrinsic part of what takes place in the normal course of events.

When the subject is organizational structure, a partnership between elected officials and senior government executives is the only possible way to create successful outcomes. If the intelligence agencies of the federal government need reorganizing, the career executives of those agencies are in a better position than anyone else to figure out how. They are the ones whose careers depend on getting things right. They are the ones properly responsible for producing the results the nation's elected officials expect. They are the ones who will work day and night trying to make the new structure a success. If they have nothing to do with shaping it, what chance will they have? The right role for future commissioners would be to help career executives design new structures and elicit political support for them.

I am not denigrating such commissions at all. These bodies can be indispensable to shaping political resolutions of large-scale problems. But these bodies cannot solve management problems. If I were wrong about this, the problems addressed by such groups would long since have been reduced in scope. It hasn't happened, and won't happen.

There is no shortage of issues and problems for elected officials at all levels of government to address. It is a constant that political time and energy are in short supply. What does not require political attention ought not to get it. With allowance for exceptions here and there, the political arena being what it is, the resolution of managerial problems can only be done by management, subject to the consent of elected officials.

Imagine if you will a private company in distress that assembled a group of distinguished former board members and presidents and sent them off to devise a new business plan with two stipulations: first, that no one in the company's management would be consulted in the process, and second, that the company's management would not

be granted authority to act on anything the group recommended. This would be laughable. But in government we
do it all the time.

Consider some examples. According to various reports, the Cancer Institute at the National Institutes of
Health "is so mired in cumbersome procedures that it
needs to be completely overhauled."[38] The Securities and
Exchange Commission's own audited statements are "in
such disarray that it had failed at some of the agency's
most fundamental tasks."[39] In February 2011 *The New
York Times* published an article identifying "30 Steps to
Better Government" based on the GAO's "updated road-
map to confronting waste, fraud, abuse, and mismanage-
ment."[40] The GAO has been issuing these reports for twenty years. The latest identifies billions of dollars in misspent
funds and uncollected taxes, fees, and charges. As always,
the report presents areas "ripe for Congress and President
Obama to take action."

Articles and reports such as these can be found in the
thousands applying to every level of government. Such reports can also be found in the thousands pertaining to business and nonprofit organizations. Such problems are not in
the least unique to government. Nor can they ever be overcome in full; it is the nature of human affairs. If we want
to move toward resolutions, we know perfectly well how to
do it. The tasks are 100% managerial and 0% political. It is
useless to study issues in one place, such as the GAO, when
the executives and managers in the agencies being studied
lack the authority and resources to solve them and have no
chance of obtaining either. We have been performing these
exercises for a very long time; if they were going to produce

institutional as opposed to political results they would have long since done so.

What Would Strong Management Do?

First, strong management would report on the "state of the organizations" for which they are responsible. They would comment on the political directions in place so their bosses could affirm or revise those directions, and they would comment on organizational successes and failures and prospects for the future. They would present elected officials with far more candid assessments than their own political appointees could ever venture to present.

Second, strong management would ask its political masters for directions with respect to the most salient questions and problems the institutions they manage face. These requests would constitute only a small subset of the universe of requests made of elected officials, but they would be vital to the institutions of government. They would not transform the directions political figures give, but they would move in the direction of coherence and clarity insofar as those institutions are concerned. The questions would be managerial in nature, not political, so that obtainable answers would lead to performance.

Among the things proposed would be overhauls of rules and administrative complexity. It would fall to management to propose the kinds of things long recommended by the Hoover Commission and other such bodies. At first this would occur within departments and agencies, but the need to deal with the larger assemblage of governmental entities would soon emerge.

Third, strong management would report on gaps between the directions they have received and institutional capabilities. Such reporting would lead to a triage process between political leaders and their managerial subordinates. It would help reduce the level of ambiguity and increase the level of clarity.

Fourth, strong management would report on the present and future cost of following directions. It is essential that these reports come from the same people who will actually manage the agencies that incur the costs. Preparing these reports would necessitate increased consultation with neutral study shops, which would benefit both operational departments and study shops. At a minimum, these reports would comply with the spirit of generally accepted accounting principles, so all involved would have a clear picture of the financial future.

Fifth, strong management would report on the productivity of the institutions they manage. This would require candid and self-critical assessments of cost-effectiveness, employee performance, contractor performance, and the state and use of equipment and property.

Sixth, strong management would look for opportunities to improve the performance of the public sector as a whole by proposing rearrangements of the larger landscape, by which I mean attending to the collective performance of government agencies rather than to just one agency at a time. This would require statesmanship in that managers would have to move outside their focus on individual agencies. It is unlikely that anyone will ask them to do so, but they must do it anyway, because their managerial values oblige them to do so. Their reward in the short term is likely to be condemnation from above and below. Over the longer term, there is no better way to demonstrate what management is about than to focus on collective performance.

These things may sound trite, but when politicians serve as their own top management they cannot perform these functions. For example, they cannot present cautionary or negative accounts that would be used by their political adversaries to challenge their competence. The reports of professional management, on the other hand, would reflect institutional realities that are independent of who holds elective office. If career professionals painted different pictures for different political masters they would be led to slaughter. This is why elected officials don't want such reports; there is potential harm but no potential benefit. It is easy to see why politicians do not want to hear bad news from people who work for them.

Yet another concern has to do with the never-ending political need to respond to demand after demand. For decades I have heard from people who work in the private sector that success there is measured by investment return, while success in government is measured by the size of budget and bureaucracy. This notion is something of a mantra for some critics of the public sector. The political arena is obliged to respond on a continuous basis to demand after demand, and evidence of such responses is abundant throughout the institutions of the public sector. Management has a different need, which is to take on a manageable number of things. Management's self-interest in this regard is entirely different from the self-interest of the political bosses. When Congress buys weapons that the military neither wants nor needs it may be good for the elected officials, but it is bad for management. This is an all too common problem.

Lastly, it is career executives' and managers' worst nightmare to be associated with administrative failures that make the front page. It embarrasses their political bosses, which is bad enough, but it also tarnishes their professional reputations and resumes. When government tries to do more than it is capable of doing well, it is rarely (I hesitate to say never) at the urging of career managers. Their interests are far better served by doing a manageable number of things that they can be seen to do well. In short, management is not a voice for "more;" it is a voice for "more effective," which is not the same thing.

Financial Viability:
The Core Management Responsibility

It is a given that the top priority for executives and managers is to serve the interests of the agencies they work for. There may and should be debate about what those interests are, and how they should be served, but there is no debate that management is about serving those interests.

This is not to say that serving those interests is necessarily a good thing. Clearly, for example, the interests of the city government I served for over thirty years were not the highest of all possible sets of interests in the larger mix of things. Moreover, as we have explored from multiple vantage points, my perspective as city manager was a limited one even within the city limits. Serving the interests of the institution I worked for was often consonant with, but never the same as, serving the interests of the city as a whole. The latter would be a far more inclusive proposition, within which the city institution would be just a small part. Even the city council's responsibilities were not inclusive of the city as a whole, as public schools were governed by separate elected boards, the county was governed by a board of supervisors, and so on. And this list omits everything outside government. So we have to be careful when we claim to know what the larger public interest might be.

As we have seen, an agency's financial success is at the top of the list of management's concerns. At the local level, this usually means building a strong tax base and establishing sets of services readily supportable by that tax base. City managers, and other local government executives and managers, focus relentlessly on that topic. I can report from experience that it is not a popular subject. Indeed, it is probable that if a city's management does not address it, no one will. It is almost invariably the case that city managers would prefer to spend less than mayors and city councils, which is the same thing as saying that city managers would prefer to spend less than the public wants spent. This is illustrative of the difference between managerial values and political values.

The connection between local economy and local government is more direct and immediate than the connection between state economies or the country's economy and those larger entities of government. For that reason local government executives and managers may be the most economically savvy and financially focused of public sector managers. As a city manager I reported to my bosses throughout my tenure that our city had established a set of services that was beyond its long-term means to fund. This is a much easier thing to say than to remedy. As hard as the economic consequences of change can be, the political consequences are often harder.

It is unfortunate that the financial interests of government agencies can be and often are served by promoting their political importance to elected officials. This reflects the underlying, fundamental axiom that political values prevail over other values. Because this is so, it is often assumed that economic merit doesn't matter. Over the long term, however, economic merit matters a great deal more than is commonly supposed. The agencies of government are in perpetual competition with each other for scarce funds. The best way for managers to prevail in this competition is to present economic evidence in support of funding. Moreover, because management will be obliged to make its case again and again over the years, to political detractors as well as supporters, it must be careful about what it says. Unverifiable claims are hazardous; management must guard against incorrect information that might produce desired outcomes today but reverse those outcomes tomorrow.

It is a given, then, that bureaucracies advance the cause of their own funding. But this hardly renders those efforts indistinguishable from politics. The plain fact of the matter is that the political arena dispenses and the managerial arena works with the results. Neither bureaucratic urgings nor management's preferences actually count for much.

While it is true that elected officials have control of the purse strings, that is not the same thing as having control over costs. The universe of costs defies both understanding and control. This is not only because of the number of agencies and the complexity of their activities, but because public sector costs are highly interdependent. We understand some of the relationships, but by no means all of them. Cutting some things produces savings, while cutting other things produces increased costs elsewhere. This is especially true when the federal government cuts back, which is often the same thing as pushing costs onto the states. The same happens inside states too, when state government reductions push costs onto local government.

Some costs can be eliminated altogether, but others cannot. This is why intending to lower or eliminate costs is not at all the same thing as achieving those results. There are too many uncertainties. For example, our country will wage war independent of the costs involved. Similarly, we may scale back government's role in health care, but we will not keep that resolve in the face of an outbreak of plague. We can repeat these observations about one public purpose after another. The truth is that our understanding of public sector cost relationships is tentative at best. The notion that any society is in charge of the costs of its existence seems highly dubious to me. In actuality we incur costs first and then we figure out how to pay for them. If elected officials were willing, we would learn that there is actually more room for management to manage costs than there is for elected officials to do it. But such a notion is politically inadmissible.

Career managers do not establish and cannot criticize the merits of the aims set forth by their elected bosses. Career managers can, however, comment on the reasonableness of the aims they are assigned in terms of the resources made available to them. Usually there are too many assignments and aims, so management is obliged to shortchange some of them. Usually there will be little political help in terms of what to shortchange. Management must nevertheless disclose what is being shortchanged, so that if the owners—the elected officials—wish to do otherwise they can. Management must also say, in its own self-interest if for no other reason, when the organizational capabilities at its disposal are inadequate to the tasks it has been directed to perform.

The concept of adequacy in terms of funding and capability invites management to expand its vision beyond given institutions into the larger whole. Management may not be able to implement revisions on its own, but it can set forth alternatives for the bosses to contemplate. Moreover, management can safely do this in language that invokes institutional rather than political values.

Managing the Workforce

If money is first and foremost, people are right behind. Every organization is dependent on the people who work there. Further, every organization is disproportionately dependent on the contributions of its most capable people. I often analogize this to Thanksgiving dinner, where many do their share but a few do much more than their share. This is the way things are always and everywhere.

As challenging as it was for me to work for elected officials, it was harder to hire and supervise department heads such as police chief, fire chief, public works director, and so on. I learned from experience to place little reliance on interviews or reference checks. Interviews are singularly unhelpful; they demonstrate no more than how well a candidate interviewed on a given day. Reference checks are only slightly more useful. The truth is that the only way to know how someone will perform at work is to hire the person and see.

Competent organizations employ the talents of their employees to advantage. They deal early on with problem employees. They develop and cultivate cultures that capable and productive people appreciate and less capable and productive people do not. Above all, they attend to outcomes. They do not blame deficient performance on administrative complexities.

The most damaging management failure of all is to accept the unacceptable in employee performance. It follows, then, that the most distinguishing attribute of successful executives and managers is that they reject the unacceptable. This may sound simple, but it isn't. There may be a few lucky managers who don't regularly face this issue, but they would have to constitute a small minority.

Consider two examples. First, the Catholic Church's failure to discharge abusive priests is a perfect manifestation of willingness to accept the unacceptable. In this case mid-management and top management not only declined to deal with performance lapses, but declined to deal with criminal conduct. Church management chose instead, over a period of decades, to move its problem and criminal employees elsewhere, in the vain hope of avoiding trouble. I cannot offer even a hint of explanation as to why any management would make such choices again and again, when they were clearly choosing the interests of individual, lower-level employees over the well-being of the institution as a whole. All we can say is that it is commonplace. This is exactly what management must not do. The Catholic Church has what would appear to be a capable hierarchy in place, but clearly it did not perform.

Second, on a lesser, noncriminal scale, school districts do the same thing when they transfer, instead of terminate, those whose teaching performance is unsatisfactory.

The same value choice is being made here: the interests of individuals are being chosen over the interests of the institution. It makes no sense to view this as anything but a management failure. Managers have a solemn obligation to place the interests of the organizations they manage above all other interests. Each individual failure to do so seems insignificant. In the aggregate, however, the consequences are grave.

For many years I have asked colleagues which choice they would make if they had the chance to either hire a superstar or say goodbye to their most problematic employee. No one has ever chosen the former. Instead, they enthusiastically tell me about how much better things would be if they could do the latter. The truth is that management can do the latter, but it is so much trouble that it happens far too little. Taken one case at a time, I don't doubt that managers make perfectly rational choices about these things. But it seems clear that management systemically underestimates the burdens their most troublesome employees create for their best employees. If management is not about performance at work it is not about anything at all.

Moreover, the acceptance of poor performance when better is available is ruinous to the institutions management serves. It is also ruinous to public employees and their labor unions.[41] Outside observers could be forgiven for thinking that most priests are child molesters and most teachers are incompetent. The truth is, of course, otherwise. The failure of management to field trustworthy priests and competent teachers on a regular, ongoing basis over the years has led to the impression that there are vast numbers of untrustworthy priests and incompetent teachers. Neither is the case, but it is too late for those facts to matter in the court of public opinion.

It is a given that executives and managers cannot achieve perfection in employee hiring and retention. There is no verifiable science about how to do this. Management can and must, however, set forth expectations and check to see if they are being met. When they are not being met, management must remedy the matter. Judgment calls have to be made. There are lots of ways to evaluate and follow through, but there is no best way. When managers are seen to fail in their responsibility to hire and retain capable employees, they must be deemed to have failed and should be replaced. There are always going to be individually challenging circumstances, but there is no good reason for widespread failures to manage.

What is so painful about this subject is that when we talk about the failings of individual employees, be they priests, teachers, or those in any other pursuit, we are talking about a very small percentage of any staff. It is not as if there is a need for management to run wild and fire vast numbers of unsuspecting employees. It is only when the responsibility to deal with the subject of performance on an individual basis is evaded for long periods of time that organizational failures loom. Simply put, it is management's job to see to it that individual failures remain individual, that they not accumulate so as to become group, and then organization-wide, failures. When management succeeds in this regard, as I would argue the cities I worked for did, no one even notices that it's happening.

Let me add, too, that not all aims can be accomplished. The degree of difficulty of the tasks at hand matters. It is futile for management to expect the impossible. Management can only apply the institutional resources it has to best advantage: the best-run institutions in the world cannot do the impossible. Institutions whose resources are inadequate to the task, as well as poorly managed institutions, are bound to fail sooner or later.

Management has the responsibility to see to it that the public's employees are focused on the right things, things that have the highest probability of successfully accomplishing the political aims at hand. Unproductive uses of time are the same as unproductive uses of money. The application of employee time, like the application of money, must be purposeful and results-oriented. This is easy to say and not at all easy to do. When people come together to work or play they develop patterns that have little to do with productive outcomes. Some of these patterns are relatively benign and others are perverse, but it is a given that they come with the territory. Knowing this, management must be clear about purposes, so everyone knows what they are about. Management must work to develop cultures of achievement.

As has so often been the case, career managers haven't enjoyed much academic support when it comes to issues of workplace cultures. Here is a remarkable academic observation: "There has been a tendency for some researchers to treat organizational culture as a 'variable' that can be controlled and manipulated like any other organizational variable...culture should (instead) be regarded as something that an organization 'is,' not something that an organization 'has': it is not an independent variable, nor can it be created, discovered, or destroyed by the whims of management."[42] I doubt that anyone who has ever been responsible for the performance of a group, much less multiple groups, would agree. Groups develop their ways; sometimes they are productive and sometimes they aren't. But management has an enormous influence on how these groups develop.

Consider the Army Corps of Engineers, one of the most notoriously bureaucratic public sector agencies. As a local government official, I worked on a single Army Corps project for thirty years. In my first year, which was year twenty-five of the project, I met for three hours with thirty Corps officials in San Francisco. The commanding general even put in an appearance. In my mind the project was straightforward enough, but for the Corps it was enormously complex. When I retired thirty years later, project construction had just been completed. One would have thought a celebration was in order. But the Corps had something else in mind: it recalculated the basic premises of the whole endeavor and changed them. The Corps thereupon set forth a whole new set of problems that needed to be solved. At this writing the matter is still in process! Unfortunately, this is not a singular incident. Every government manager can tell horror stories of agencies and departments with counterproductive cultures.

Fortunately, such horror stories are not typical of government as a whole. I would argue that the institutions of government perform rather well for the most part. In fact, the worst cases receive much more attention than their actual numbers would justify. It is unfortunate but inevitable that the prevailing view of government institutions will to a large extent be based on those worst cases. Things done right are not newsworthy.

While worst case examples provide the best illustrations of the need for management, it would be foolish to say that management is only required when things have gone badly. Contrary to what some academic observers say, management is about establishing cultures of performance and fighting against cultures that impede performance. It is a never-ending activity, because people seem to be endowed with a special genius for creating counter-productive cultures. They are everywhere to be found. Moreover, people defend them zealously. Management must constantly be about the promotion of productive and managerial values and the rejection of norms and practices that impede.

Peter Drucker wrote that "Managers are the basic resource of the business enterprise…How well managers manage and are managed determines whether business goals will be reached. It also largely determines how well the enterprise manages worker and work."[43] Drucker goes on to observe that, despite exhortations that top management and middle management should focus "downwards" on the organization chart, what people actually do in the real world is focus upwards. In business, this upward focus is on top management. Because there is so little top management in government, upward focus is largely without reward. In theory, government's employees should look upward to elected officials. But they are not looking back. The only possible way to meet the need for purpose and clarity signified by the natural impulse to look upwards is for employees to look to management.

Asset Management

The public, through its government, owns an abundance of property, plant, and equipment. It is management's job to serve as custodian of these assets. It is clear that more is owned than can be responsibly managed and afforded. Everywhere we turn we face increasing financial liabilities related to the public's assets. If government were to put a value on these assets, they would be substantial indeed: we would look rich. But for the most part there is no one to sell them to, and they are not for sale anyway. So they constitute financial liabilities instead.

Management cannot magically produce the money and other resources it would require to become responsible owners of all that is owned. It can, however, report on the condition of these assets to the elected officials who are the owners. Auto repair shop ads frequently say, "You can spend a little now or more later." This is the underlying axiom of ownership. It is almost always less expensive to maintain what is owned than not to. Concerning the need to spend millions of dollars resurfacing the city's streets, one of the city councilmembers I worked for put it this way: "We don't have a street problem so much as a financial problem. I do not want to spend this much on streets, but if we don't resurface them now we will have to rebuild them later and that would cost five times more."

The nation's elected officials face the difficult–indeed almost impossible—task of choosing what shall be maintained and what shall not. But the results of these choices can rarely be acknowledged. There are no politicians in support of bridges that fall down or water treatment plants that cannot produce potable water. There are only different degrees of risk that politicians are willing to take in these situations. If every bridge in the country were ready to fall down tomorrow, it would be easy to vote for repairs. The situation is analogous to the need for a new roof. Roofs with the potential to leak and roofs that are actually leaking are two different things. There is little or no political reward for dealing with the former, but clear reward for dealing with the latter. There are thousands of examples of this problem at every level of government. Despite the inherent political aversion to dealing with problems that have not yet become acute, it is a fundamental management responsibility to provide full disclosure of what needs to be spent to achieve the lowest long-term costs of ownership.

Finally, management must apply the limited funds at its disposal to best advantage, and be clear about the assumptions it has made and the choices it recommends. This sounds like a simple matter, but it is no such thing. The need to maintain some things, such as highways, bridges, and river levees, is straightforward. What is required for other things, such as nuclear weapons, hazardous waste dumps, and the like, is not so clear.

The time-honored system for public works contracts is one of competitive bidding. At all levels of government, public managers are required by law to award contracts to the lowest responsible bidders. These competitive processes are supposed to serve two purposes: obtaining advantageous prices and ensuring openness. Not surprisingly, things don't always work out that way. I used to cynically observe that when cities award contracts to low bidders they are actually choosing two things, the firm that will do the work and the one they will see in court later on when things go awry.

The problem is a simple one, and known to every government manager. In a competitive environment the low bid will often turn out to be unprofitable for the low bidder. This obliges the low bidder to find discrepancies between the bid documents on which they based their bid and what turns out to be required in the actual course of construction. There are always variances between the two, because it is impossible to write specifications that contemplate every eventuality, so there are always opportunities for change orders.

This is why the real competition for price often doesn't take place in the formal bidding process, but in the battles over change orders that take place during construction. Government managers know that when public agencies make bid awards at bid prices they are at the beginning, not the end, of the price-setting process. They are also at the beginning of the project definition process, because only the simplest projects turn out as anticipated. (Think of kitchen remodeling.)

When professional managers contract for professional services, on the other hand, they are not obliged to choose by price alone; they can take into account a full range of factors and make judgments about which competitors would serve best. I would argue that, in the absence of evidence to the contrary, there is equal potential for abuse in both approaches, but greater potential for success when professional managers are in charge because they can make choices. Moreover, it is doubtful that the low-bid system saves the public money. There are times and places when low-bid processes are undoubtedly the best choice, but there are other times and places when it isn't. I would never argue to reduce the openness of the selection process, but I would argue for more management discretion in making bid awards with the public's money.

Because it is impossible to afford even the lowest-cost efforts for everything that is owned government has to perform triage and identify which assets will not be tended to. Because this is how management nightmares become political nightmares, this must be carefully done. While politicians are obliged to claim managerial prowess, few of them would claim to be expert at the financial equations of ownership. Management must take the lead.

It may well be that, if the profession of management is ever admitted to the federal government, it will start with asset management. I say this in the hope that a widely recognized success story will someday be seen as a precursor of management. The example is BRAC, the Defense Department's Base Closure and Realignment Commission.

This Commission was established for exactly the same reason that government first retained nonpatronage employees: there was no alternative. In this case, the Defense Department had "experienced difficulty in closing military bases to match the requirements of downsized forces with changed composition. During the decade of the 1980s, major military base closures were seriously hampered by procedural requirements established by Congress, *to the point that none occurred* [emphasis added]. The mismatch between real estate assets and defense requirements grew with the military downsizing that began late in the Reagan Administration and continued under Presidents George H. W. Bush and Clinton."[44] In other words, the Defense Department could not obtain Congressional consent for acting in accordance with Congress's own instructions. It is a common enough problem, but in this case it rose to a level that obliged Congress to forge a remedy.

The BRAC process began in 1988 with the establishment of a bipartisan commission, the members of which were appointed by the Secretary of Defense for the purpose of recommending base closures. The process further established that Congress would approve or reject the Commission's recommendations but not modify them. The process worked well enough that it was repeated. Under the current model, Commissioners are appointed by the President, who must approve the Commission's recommendations before they are submitted to Congress for approval or rejection. If the President rejects the recommendations, the process is terminated.

Seen from the glass half-full perspective, the BRAC approach enables the Department of Defense to submit management-minded recommendations to Congress and have those recommendations approved or rejected but not micromanaged. Seen through glass half-empty lenses, it is just another example of the political avoidance of management. Both perspectives are valid.

In a May 14, 2011 article, the *Federal Times*[45] proposed a "Civilian BRAC" to address the subject of non-military surplus properties. The article's author, David Baxa, who is also the President of a company that supports planning and implementation of Army BRAC-related activities, argued that a civilian BRAC "would go a long way toward better using federal assets with major cost savings in the bargain."[46] There can be no doubt that Mr. Baxa is correct, that a civilian BRAC-like process would be a vast improvement over the way things are done and have always been done.

That the notion of a government-wide BRAC-type

process can be aired in public in a prestigious publication may be auspicious. At the same time, the underlying assumption behind every such commission process (which is that a special mechanism outside the normal operation of government is required because Congress intends that something actually be accomplished) is embarrassing and nonsensical. Asset management is a fundamental management responsibility. It would be better if government's managers were not just allowed, but required, to do their jobs. Still, it would be a good thing if the BRAC process is a harbinger of things to come in terms of moving away from political rigidity and toward managerial flexibility.

The Clear and Compelling Need for Managerial Statesmanship

We come at last to the biggest subject of all: the need to re-engineer, if you will, the myriad institutions of government into a more manageable whole. We are a young country, but because we grew at breakneck speed the landscape of government entities is more reflective of the needs of the past than those of the present. I feel confident that almost no one with a passing knowledge of the public sector would disagree with this statement. But there has never been anyone to deal with it. Every elected and managerial official in the country is attached to an existing institution or set of institutions. No one has any responsibility whatsoever to rearrange them for any reason. Moreover, when the need for a particular rearrangement becomes acutely compelling and someone advocates it, more often than not it provokes a vicious and negative response. Anyone in a position to see what ought to be done—that is, anyone with experience and expertise—is also in a position to know that the prospects of success are small and the probability of being pilloried high. Let me give one small-scale example of what I mean.

I have lived and worked in California's smallest county (in area) for over thirty years. One of its most obviously inefficient attributes is that fire protection services are provided by thirteen fire departments. One or two at the most would do the job better in every respect. The structure in place is wholly vestigial; it makes no contemporary sense at all. For some reason (my daughter would say it was because I am stubborn and don't care what people say about me) I decided to take on the subject as a sort of extracurricular endeavor. For decades I advocated consolidation on the basis of cost-effectiveness and performance. Once we came very close to consolidating two of those departments, but in the end it fell apart. Over those decades I recruited a few elected officials, and a few fire professionals, to the task, but that was all. Neither the press nor the public was the slightest bit interested in the structure of the fire service, the management of the fire service, or anything having to do with those things. If people had been dying, or if fires had not been responded to, or if other egregious and newsworthy events had taken place, there might have been flickers of interest, lasting until something more interesting occurred. The subjects of structure, performance, cost-effectiveness, and the like are managerial subjects. They are not political subjects, and they are rarely newsworthy subjects. This is the underlying reality anyone interested in those things has to face and overcome.

We pay lip service but little more to reports like those of the Hoover Commission and the California Constitutional Revision panel. Hundreds and perhaps even thousands of such reports have been issued over the decades. They consistently produce almost zero political traction, for the reason that political values have little to do with managerial values. The concerns of politicians accurately reflect the concerns of the public, and managerial values are not among them.

In times like the present, when the economy is sour and the costs of government feel out of control, political momentum builds behind the notion that all political inputs of the past, and the institutions of government as a whole, must be repudiated and slashed in punishment for their failure to achieve cost-effectiveness. All at once the public sector's shortcomings are center stage, and a reckoning is demanded. No doubt there will be reckonings at all levels of government. But we have short attention spans, and we want to fix the problems overnight and then not hear about them anymore. Slashing costs, even if that is done, won't change the landscape at all; indeed, it will only make what is actually needed more necessary and less likely.

If it were possible for well-meaning elected officials to reengineer the landscape of the public sector it would long since have been done. Every elected official in the country knows that there is much to do. But it cannot be done by elected officials, because they hold political office and can at best solve political problems. They cannot solve managerial problems. The structure and cost-effectiveness of government are managerial issues, and can only be addressed by professional management.

Our country needs a massive dose of statesmanship

from its professional government executives and managers at all levels. These people need to move beyond serving the interests of the departments and agencies they work for, survey the landscape in their areas of expertise, and develop proposals to reorganize and restructure the public sector. No one else can do this. These professionals, however, surely can.

The public interest, and in the long run the interests of those who work for government, would be served by greatly reducing the number of governmental entities, clarifying their purposes, and refocusing on performance. Now more than ever, when we are cutting everything but reshaping nothing, we must reshape. And as we have seen, this is managerial, not political, work. The political need to cut budgets will come to an end at some point, but the need to manage government will endure. If we were to admit management to the public sector's institutions and not only allow but promote the application of managerial values over the longer term, we could move steadily closer to the productive visions that studies of government always set forth.

Government career executives and managers should take this on for a multitude of reasons. First, it is in their self-interest to do so, because they cannot flourish if the institutions they manage are under siege and floundering. It will be better for all government employees, not just executives and managers, to have a smaller number of successful units than a larger number that are not successful. Second, pride is a powerful motivator. The professional executives and managers I have known over the decades have all taken pride in their work and the work of their colleagues. But it has never been the case that they could be proud of the larger universe of numerous departments and managerial levels. In their self-interest they must extend the reach of their pride to the bigger picture. Although they are sure to make enemies doing this, it should only reinforce how worthwhile it would be. Third, they have a moral obligation to propose and recommend what is needed, whether or not they have been asked to do so.

Proposals to move in these directions will have to be accompanied by grants of authority to act if results are to be achieved. The handcuffs, leg irons, and straightjackets must come off. Executives and managers must be given room to perform. This must include room to change, within reasonable limits, government's rules and structures. The need for performance does not begin anew after every election; it is continuous. Politicians must learn to judge the performance of their managements instead of engaging in the pretense of acting as top management themselves.

There is lots of low-hanging fruit, as it were, for career managers to gobble up. They will not be allowed to fundamentally rearrange the landscape. But the urgent political need to save money presents a fine opportunity to look beyond individual institutions. Career managers everywhere need to seek out like-minded colleagues and pursue big-picture, cost-saving, productivity-generating measures. If they are rejected, so be it. If they are not proposed, there is zero chance for change. The vast majority of measures that would fall in the category of low-hanging fruit will never be proposed by elected officials, but could very well be proposed by career managers. And success with low-hanging fruit might even lead to reaching higher.

The Cost of Management

It is fair to ask whether or not current salaries are adequate to this strong management proposition and if there is sufficient talent already inside government to meet the need. Unfortunately, I don't know the answer. We have no experience to guide us. My own observations and experience lead me to think that there would not have to be wholesale salary increases to attract capable managers to the jobs. In fact, positions with the authority to manage might be attractive enough in and of themselves. It is certain that the top management salaries we see in the private sector are unnecessary.[47] At most, some additional compensation might be required, and would be in order. For the most part, government has about the right number of positions in the top ranks, they are just woefully lacking in authority. The need for new positions would be modest.

Whatever the exact answers to these questions might turn out to be, the cost of management's absence is far greater than the cost of its presence would be. Over the long term, greatly strengthened management would not cost anything at all—it would add value. In the short term top executives and managers already earn the highest incomes found in the public sector (there are a few exceptions, but it is a valid generalization), and it would add to budgets to increase their numbers and/or their pay. However, because management's job is to manage costs, obtain savings, and achieve cost-effectiveness, successful managers more than pay for themselves over time.

The economic value of management became increasingly evident to me as the city I managed made round after round of budget cuts in response to the Recession of

2007. During each round of cuts, there were calls to cut or eliminate the management. We did a fair amount of that too, out of a sense of fairness and balance as well as political necessity. But over and over again top and middle managers came up with one inspiration after another. Every time I thought there was no more of it to be had, they proved me wrong. If this is so at the local level, and it is, there is far, far more for management to accomplish in the higher and larger entities of government.

The following proposition is open to analysis, but I would wager that city manager cities have reduced spending and reshaped themselves with far fewer adverse effects on outcomes than other government agencies. I would further wager that the single most important factor in terms of the long-term viability of the wrenching changes being made in public sector institutions as a whole is the quality of the management. But we would have to have a performance-oriented academy and performance-oriented journalists to know for sure.

It is embedded in the nature of things that there are always ways to improve performance. There are also good and bad ways to realize savings. These are never-ending propositions. The political approach has historically been to establish political bodies (such as the Hoover Commission) to make one-time recommendations and then be done with these matters. The current political way is to slash spending everywhere, across the board. The managerial way is to continuously attend to performance and cost-effectiveness as a never-ending endeavor. This is the only way to achieve long-term results.

What Management Can and Cannot Do

Management cannot solve political problems or perform political functions. It cannot appropriate funds, set tax rates, or even advise its political masters about solving political problems. Career managers are not about elections, speaking for the people, speaking for the government, setting the public's priorities, or resolving political issues. The political arena is for politicians and the political class; management is prohibited from entering.

It might be tempting to think that since making policy eludes politicians, perhaps management could provide it. But trying would only cause political trouble. It is fair, however, for management to point out what things cost, although cost information may or may not be welcome. Management has to be careful about expressing approval or disapproval of costs, but does not have to be reticent about revealing them. When managers do so, they may find themselves uncomfortably close to the political arena, which explains why management is often reluctant to be forthcoming about costs.

Consider a tendentious example. California is experiencing a colossal budget crisis, like many other states, and is slashing expenditures in almost every function. At the same time, a federal court has assumed jurisdiction over California's prisons, having ruled that the deplorable conditions often found there are unconstitutional. Would it, or would it not, be appropriate for management to point out the cost of implementing life sentences, under California's three-strikes law, for inmates who are guilty of no more than petty crimes? One inmate, whose case went to the U.S. Supreme Court, is serving fifty years, at a cost to the State of $50,000 per year, for committing three petty thefts of less than $100 each.[48] Perhaps three hundred people are in this category. The State of California went to a great deal of cost and effort to protect its right to impose such sentences, and the U.S. Supreme Court supported that right. Does management dare raise the issue of cost-effectiveness in such circumstances?

There is no clear answer to this question. It seems to me that when new circumstances apply, career managers are obliged to ask their bosses to revisit prior decisions. Clearly it is not for management to decide whether or not long and expensive sentences should be imposed for petty offenses. On the other hand, it is clearly appropriate for prison management to present cost data to elected officials. It is appropriate for prison management to report on employee workload, the condition of facilities, and a host of other concerns. If prisoners are going to be released on court order or as a result of budget cuts, it is surely appropriate for management to recommend how best to reduce the number of prisoners being held. Justice, as it were, is for elected officials, but costs and operations are well within the purview of management. This is hardly a unique example: the public sector's managers face analogous problems every day. Managers know full well how to present these issues in tactful and deferential form, though they can hardly expect their reports to be welcome.

If it is true that management cannot solve political problems, the reverse is also true: politicians cannot solve managerial problems. Politicians rarely even set foot in the offices, or even the buildings, where management is done. Politicians typically have little experience or expertise in any of the functions of bureaucracy. Politicians can no more accomplish managerial objectives inside the departments of government than managers can accomplish political objectives. Politicians are not prohibited from trying, but they might as well be.

Management in Disregard

A confluence of management failures has created worldwide turmoil. To cite just a few huge examples, management failures on Wall Street and in the banking industry nearly caused a worldwide depression. Management failures at Fannie Mae and Freddie Mac, aided and abetted by political authorities, together with the Federal Reserve's commitment to low interest rates and declination to worry about a housing bubble, made the near collapse ever so much worse. A management failure by BP Oil produced a monstrous oil spill in the Gulf of Mexico. Even more recently, a long list of failures on the part of Tokyo Electric Power and its nuclear power plant at Fukushima Daiichi produced the worst nuclear accident since Chernobyl. If my goal were to make a very long list of such failures, it would not be hard to do.

Management is deservedly in a state of disrepute. The private sector, which is supposed to be a showcase of management and organizational performance, has visited one failure after another on an unsuspecting public. Large swaths of the private sector, which is supposed to be grounded in economic reality, proved indifferent to it instead. One could be forgiven for thinking that private sector management is anything but a force for public good.[49]

We have come to equate successful management with profitability, but surely that is wrong. Management is about organizational performance, which is highly compatible with but nevertheless different from profit. Sometimes poorly functioning organizations are profitable, even over the long term, and sometimes well-functioning organizations are unprofitable. Peter Drucker knew this full well, which is why he urged executives above all other things to seek understanding of the larger purposes and long-term potential of their enterprises. Capable managers are about organizational performance; profit is often, but not always, a result. Profit, after all, is generated by the conduct of people outside business enterprises, over whom businesses have no control. What business management really does is perform as well as it can and hope that the results will be to customers' liking.

The public sector, which has never featured much in the way of management, has been a showcase for the unrestrained application of political priorities. Those priorities, like so many of their private sector counterparts, were also pursued independent of economic reality. Government demonstrated that political values took priority over economic values.

Comeuppance has come to all. A little humility would be an appropriate response. Curiously, however, we seem to be experiencing the death of humility instead. In such a climate the moderate, restrained, focused perspectives of management are unlikely to gain ascendency.

Nevertheless, we live in a world of organizations large and small. The successes and failures of the future will to a very large degree be those of organizations. Every one of them requires management. It is not auspicious that in the first part of the twenty-first century management has performed so badly in so many ways. But there is no alternative to management. We will have to learn to do better, in both the private sector and in the public sector.

The public sector's institutions desperately need performance-oriented management. Politicians may fear that this would diminish them. But the opposite is true. Strong management would be an asset to strong politicians. Strong political leadership and strong managerial structures are not only entirely compatible, they are essential, both of them. Moreover, the public sector is at no risk of the management excesses that have taken place in the private sector because, as we have seen, the fact that career managers will report tomorrow to the political adversaries of those they report to today serves as a guarantee against it.

It is in order to acknowledge the obvious, which is that competent management is not so easy to obtain. Incompetent management is all too common. Humans, including executives and managers, are just not that good. Competence, in human affairs generally and in organizations in particular, is not abundant; it has to be cultivated. (I have long thought, perhaps perversely, that Tom Peters should have written *In Search of Competence* instead of *In Search of Excellence*.)

A fundamental question, one that is beyond the scope of this book, emerges from such an acknowledgment: what is the best way to check up on management, both public and private, to promote desired outcomes, and guard against catastrophic failures? Around the world we are seeing outcomes that showcase the inadequacies of both unregulated and regulated activities. If we knew how to obtain responsible private sector management, we would need little in the way of public sector regulation. The notion that market forces will somehow in and of themselves produce responsible management is clearly folly. Alternatively, if we knew how to regulate successfully, the private sector's management failures wouldn't matter so much. We don't know how to regulate successfully either.

There will be no panaceas. But it makes no more sense to abandon management because of its failures than it would make to abandon medicine, or any other field, as a result of its failures. As long as we are going to have institutions, which will be as long as humans live, we will require management. The failures management has visited upon us demonstrate its critical importance. Competent management may elude us forever, but its pursuit is essential. That is especially so in terms of public institutions, which trail their private counterparts in the development of management.

In a bold rethinking of what has made Western economies richer and more successful than others, in particular those of the Middle East, Timur Kuran argues that, above all other things, the creation of commercial institutions accounts for the differences. Mr. Kuran says that Western societies and traditions were uniquely able to produce commercial institutions capable of mobilizing large quantities of productive resources and of enduring over time.[50]

In *Why Nations Fail*, Daron Acemoglu and James A. Robinson focus on both private and public sector institutions. They argue that rich and successful societies are characterized by "inclusive," as opposed to "extractive," institutions, including business and government institutions. "Inclusive" institutions engage broadly with society, reflecting and responding to them, rather than simply imposing upon them, as the narrow elites that preceded them did. The "inclusive institutions" of the developed world have been in the making for three hundred years. Such institutions cannot be planted at will and expected to thrive. More particularly, as far as government is concerned, the authors argue that "pluralism, the cornerstone of inclusive political institutions, requires political power to be widely held in society," which also does not take place in the short term.[51]

Acemoglu and Robinson refer to the institutions of government in the world's democracies as "political institutions." Perhaps the next step in the progression of thinking that led to these recent books will be to divide the concept of "political institutions" into two parts: the first being the practice of politics and the second the performance of government institutions.

It is highly plausible that the management of government matters much more than we know. Everything I have witnessed in my own experience tells me that this is the case. If we want government to perform better in the future the only plausible route is through strengthened management. We must abandon the notion that management is for the private sector only.

Thinking Through Management Responsibilities

The most formidable responsibility facing career public sector executives and managers, individually and collectively, is to compensate for the absence of top management. Of course, caution is in order. Career people cannot, must not, and dare not, fill the top management void themselves, by stealth or any other means. In other words, they must recognize and deal with, not remedy, the structural inadequacy at the top. The structural inadequacy at the top cannot be remedied until politicians choose to remedy it.

Their second responsibility is to compensate for the weakness of middle management. The caution that applies to the top management void does not apply to the middle. Middle managers are mightily constrained, to be sure, but they have more in the way of opportunity than those at the top. Managers in the middle must identify and act on those opportunities.

We have seen that the political values of those serving as owners of the institutions of government supersede all other values. This is clear and given. We have also seen that career executives and managers are obliged to invoke and apply managerial values as the highest set of values, as long as they do not conflict with prevailing political values. Put another way, when values other than political ones come into conflict with managerial values, career executives and managers must act in accordance with managerial values. It is not good enough to apply managerial values only when it is convenient, because it is almost never convenient.

The best way for career executives and managers to begin compensating for the absence of top management is to ask themselves what their agencies and departments would be like if, from the time of their establishment, strong and capable top management had been in place. What would be different? What would be the same? The same questions must be asked in terms of middle management as well.

The purpose of asking these questions is to elicit *thinking*. Career executives must (and career managers should) think like top management even if they cannot act like top management. Executives must know, across the spectrum from broad purposes to detailed implementation, what they would do if they were suddenly blessed with reasonable measures of authority. Managers must do the same in the middle, which is harder because the management voids at the top are more readily apparent than those in the middle. It is easy and fun to imagine what should be done at the top. The process of thinking about the middle, however, requires managers to subordinate professional and cultural values, which are abundant, to managerial, performance values, which are not absent but are less abundant. This leads in turn to thinking about all the things that are not as they should be, and how to make them so.

A reasonably sound understanding of the big picture is a prerequisite to this exercise. Most public sector employees, like people everywhere, are immersed in the particulars of their work. They can provide edifying reports about the microcosms they know. But it is much harder to obtain perspective on the big picture. Employees do not come to work to deal with the big picture. Even executives who report directly to elected officials, or perhaps especially those executives, have little if any time to focus on big-picture understanding. It is the same for everyone in every line of work. Doctors address the ills of individual patients, not the larger public health; contractors build individual buildings, not cities. Every day the urgent pushes out the less urgent, making it nearly impossible to focus on bigger-picture matters.

Even when managers are able to focus on the big picture, understanding it is always a work in progress; it is never achieved. Perhaps it would be better to say that top management must be about the pursuit of understanding rather than understanding itself. Regardless, everyone who works for an organization wants to know what the people at the top are thinking and planning.

No two people will form the same big-picture view, nor should they. But one factor is foundational and must be thought through: the indispensability of the institution(s) being addressed. Indispensability no doubt comes in degrees; one person's essential is another's dispensable. Nevertheless, we cannot formulate a larger understanding without acknowledging that the public is mandated to pay for the public sector's services, and that this creates a unique set of responsibilities and obligations.

Successful contemplation will also require a rigorous application of judgment in terms of performance and outcomes. No other terms are allowed. One must, in this intellectual exercise at least, be open to doubting the merits of one's job, department, and agency. One must be prepared to admit to oneself, if not to anyone else, how and what things would be different if performance were the salient value.

This process must be started by individuals, because career executives and managers have not been asked, and will not be asked, to contemplate any such things. Still, in order to perform effectively in their subordinate roles, they must know what they would do were they not subordinate. They must think about every issue as though it were theirs to decide. This is the only way to produce responsible recommendations to the owners and owners' representatives they work for, and to effectively manage and supervise those who report to them. They also need to know because sometimes, usually as a matter of pure chance, opportunities present themselves and only the prepared can take advantage of them.

Imagine, for the sake of conceptualizing public sector management's burdens, how a corporation's management would respond if it worked for a board that: 1) was elected by the public, 2) appointed its own top management staff after each election, 3) was obliged to hold and pursue reelection as the top goal, and 4) was obliged to view corporate performance primarily, if not exclusively, in terms of election results. Such a structure would make life exponentially more difficult but would hardly obviate the need for corporate management. It would oblige corporate management to enunciate its purposes and values in order to fit them together in the best manner possible with those of the board members and their appointees. This is what the public sector's management must do: think through and articulate the intrinsic needs of the institutions for which they bear management responsibility and communicate them to the members of the political class they work for.

The key to thinking as top management is to focus first on big-picture results. We have seen that almost no one in government is actually called upon to do this. It is therefore a perfectly legitimate activity for management to undertake. Indeed, it is a mandatory activity. Unfortunately, in the real world, even thinking about organizational success can be heretical. So it has to be carefully and thoughtfully done in the context of managerial, and never in the context of political, values. My experience tells me that understanding the big picture is a prerequisite to managerial success. Absent understanding, it is impossible to devise means of achieving success or avoiding catastrophe. The pursuit of understanding, then, must be integral to everything that an organization does. And the more widely this pursuit is undertaken the better.

Most organizations and most executives have too many top priorities. It is best to have one or two. Three is more than most organizations or individuals can handle. Priorities beyond three must be relegated to the middle, where it is unavoidable that there will be dozens or more. But selecting the right top priorities is a frightening responsibility. It is so much easier to have a plethora of them than to select one, two, or three. Moreover, the more top priorities there are the less likely it is that explanations will be required for leaving something off the list. At the same time, the more top priorities there are the less coherent and capable the response to each of them will be. Top management has to choose. And it has to tell everyone what its choices are. Top management's choices must be compatible with political rule. These priorities, however, are not for the owners, but for the employees. Properly established, they should not—indeed, they must not—occasion political upset.

Every executive and manager should have a personal list of the top-management decisions he would make if he could. It should be constantly reviewed and modified. Such lists serve to keep their creators attentive to the big things at hand. They are intrinsic to the process of thinking things through, as inevitably they will start to contain contradictions, not to mention impossibilities. But long lists are unlikely to be helpful, because at best only a small number of big things can be accomplished. Regular list triage is therefore essential.

Because it will do no good for individual managers

to keep their thoughts to themselves, they must share their well-developed thinking with colleagues. They can do this safely so long as they stand on managerial ground. Thinking and talking about managerial values, which is to say thinking about organizational performance and success, must become an integral part of what takes place at work.

Each manager's list should include three kinds of items. The first is structural: how would we organize if we were free to decide. Almost invariably fewer and simpler structures will be called for. The issues covered in this category will be those addressed by the Hoover Commission and other similar reports over the years (at all levels of government). The second is operational: how should we operate those structures? And the third concerns plant and equipment: given the almost universal financial inability to care for what is owned, what should be done?

Preparing these lists is an exercise in thought, not in report writing, much less in preparing PowerPoint presentations. When I worked in city government I always had a complete picture of my answers in my head, but I also maintained a written version that fit on a credit card-sized piece of paper. My purpose, after all, was to keep myself focused on the big picture and prepared to act if the opportunity arose. Although, as noted, the items on the list fall into three categories, the list is still a big-picture exercise. It is no good to get bogged down.

In order to accomplish anything career executives who report to elected officials and their appointees have to engage with those authorities and invite them into the management arena, as it were. This is the opposite of what happens in the usual course of events. Some elected officials will be interested and supportive and others will not. Career executives have to take what they can get and do as much as they can with it. This means that career people have to overcome their natural wariness of political figures: the idea of inviting them to share management's headaches is not thought of as a headache remedy.

The unfortunate fact of the matter, as we have taken note of over and over again, is that few elected officials, and few of their appointees, have time for the management arena even if they have interest in it. The best possible result for career executives is to obtain cautious consent for acting on a select number of management priorities. Sometimes that will be enough to accomplish something big and worth accomplishing. More often, modest things will be sanctioned. Even when nothing is accomplished, consultation with the owners about the salient items from the management arena will have taken place, discharging management's responsibility to do so.

A few elected officials, and some of their appointees, will be management-oriented and therefore open and receptive to management's problems and priorities. These people may or may not have the means of persuading their colleagues of the importance of those problems and priorities. If anyone is going to do so, however, they are the ones. They may also become known as the ones to go to on management matters, so their importance can be disproportionate to their numbers.

Experience tells me that the best way for career executives to approach the elected officials and political appointees they report to is to recognize the differences in values and perspectives they bring to their work. When career executives set forth their managerial values and objectives, and acknowledge that those values and objectives are subordinate to the political values at hand, they are a lot less threatening than would otherwise be the case. If political consent cannot be obtained, there is nothing to be done about it. The owners have the full and unfettered right to reject management's values and priorities.

Purposes and Performance

Purposes are for elected officials only. It is in the nature of things political that there will be a multitude of purposes. From time to time there may be retrenchments, but modern society is too complex and variable for government to be simple and fixed. New purposes emerge every day, and elected officials have no choice but to respond to them. The plethora of government entities and purposes is irrefutable evidence to this effect.

Thinking about purposes reveals what is perhaps the most fundamental divide between the values of elected officials and career managers. The well-being of elected officials is subject to elections, which obliges them to respond to the immediate needs and demands of the people. The well-being of career officials is tied to organizational performance. The former dictates that myriad needs be addressed. The latter dictates that a smaller number of needs be addressed satisfactorily. This value divide cannot be resolved; it can only be recognized.

It is an underlying, fundamental political reality that the agencies of government will, everywhere and always, be directed to do more than it is possible for them to do. That is why it is also an underlying, fundamental management reality that career executives and managers must constantly advise their bosses that they lack the money, time, people, equipment, and whatever else is required to successfully do all that they have been directed to do. This is why city managers as a group are seen as curmudgeons, always raining on elected officials' parades. Because new political demands are, one at a time, too minor to matter very much, they are readily added to the landscape at the behest of elected officials. Later, when the list of things to be done is too long, the backlog is management's problem.

Career managers are truly stuck. At the local level, management is directed to hire more police officers and firefighters and build more parks and schools than can be afforded because people demand them, and because the costs at the outset are far less than they will be in the end. We do the same at the state and federal levels, only on a far larger scale. Management cannot, on its own authority, abandon anything; only elected officials can do that. So instead of deleting things, when cutbacks are required, we shrink everything instead. This further exaggerates the original public sector condition, which is an excess of purposes and an inadequacy of means to address them.

Observing these things yet again brings us back to the top management function of creating coherent organizational wholes. Management cannot establish political purposes, but must issue directions in pursuit of those purposes. Management translates the words and actions of political bosses into organizationally useful terms. As much as possible, management tries to persuade politicians to give directions that lend themselves to being accomplished. Management must do this without offending sensibilities across the political spectrum and without creating public consternation.

Career executives and managers have no choice but to conceptualize, refine, and promote workable outcomes, from the organizational standpoint, that have a chance to endure. Doing this fulfills their duty to the organizations and the political masters they serve. Management has to be ahead of the political curve in this regard, even if it cannot shape political outcomes. Management has to know what the institutional landscape would look like in the event of a wide variety of possible future political outcomes. Management is obliged to redefine issues in ways that lend themselves to organizational response.

Career executives and managers must bear two big things in mind at all times, and constantly remind their political bosses of these things. The first is a negative in that "Large organizations cannot be versatile...an organization, no matter what it would like to do, can only do a small number of tasks at any one time. This is not something that better organization or 'effective communications' can cure."[52] Management is about using the resources at its disposal to produce the best possible outcomes. If management's bosses, not to mention those who work for management, fail to understand what is possible and efficacious—and what is not—achievement will be impossible.

The second big thing is a positive in that "No organization which purposefully and systematically abandons the unproductive and obsolete ever wants for opportunities. Ideas are always around in profusion."[53] Creativity is not an attribute commonly associated with public institutions, but it is there in abundance. The way to tap it is through relentless pursuit of better outcomes and relentless resistance to the continuation of the status quo. Management is the only possible initiator.

At present it appears that the salient management challenge of the future will be to execute unprecedented cutbacks in public sector spending and activities. Because the reductions will very likely reach far beyond the boundaries of individual institutions, management must be ready to work with colleagues in departments and agencies previously unknown to them to design new, more cost-effective configurations. These will not be popular. Career executives and managers will have to reshape the landscape of public institutions to conform to both political and economic reality. They are used to doing the former, but not the latter. Indeed, they have mostly been told not to worry about the latter. But that time is over. Management must develop and present coherent and far-reaching institutional changes to the elected officials to whom they report.

Because the current economic downturn is shaping the public sector in new and unprecedented ways, government's elected officials and career managers are being called upon to account for economic results that they never had to account for before. It is plainly evident that we are not at all accustomed to thinking about the institutions of government in terms of economic outcomes. In the next and concluding section, I will attempt to scratch the surface of this subject.

Endnotes

1 Peter F. Drucker, *Management: Tasks, Responsibilities, Practices* (New York: Harper & Row, 1993), 387.

2 Peter F. Drucker, *The Age of Discontinuity* (New York: Harper & Row, 1992), 212.

3 Ibid., 222.

4 Ibid., 232.

5 Ibid., 235.

6 Finer, *History of Government*, 64.

7 My family has a saying that applies: "Face the facts before the facts face you."

8 Finer, *History of Government*, 64.

9 Fukuyama, *The Origins of Political Order*, quoted in *The Economist*, April 2, 2011, 79.

10 Philip Klein, "ASCME Union is 'Big Dog' in 2010 Campaign Spending," *American Spectator,* http://spectator.org/blog/2010/10/22/public-sector-union (accessed 7/10/11).

11 Frank Gervasi, *Big Government: The Meaning and Purpose of the Hoover Commission Report* (New York: McGraw-Hill Book Company, 1949), 18.

12 Chapter 19, "The Report of the Commission on Organization of the Executive Branch of Government, Excerpts from the Hoover Commission," in *Classics of Public Administration,* edited by Jay M. Shafritz and Albert C.

Hyde (Ft. Worth, TX: Harcourt Brace College Publishers, 1997), 154.

13   Ibid., 33.

14   California Constitutional Revision Report, accessed 1/20/2010, found at www.californiacityfinance.com/ccrcfi-nalrpt.pdf, 1994-96, iii.

15   Ibid., 71.

16   Drucker, *Age of Discontinuity*, 230.

17   Over the years I received countless surveys from graduate students in public administration pursuing advanced degrees. Almost all these surveys asked me to rank competing priorities with regard to one subject or another; the end product would compare and contrast the universe of survey responses. No one ever inquired about managerial performance.

18   I want to express my thanks to Marilena Amoni, recently retired career federal executive with the National Highway Traffic Safety Administration, who talked to me at length about her experiences on March 8, 2012.

19   I also want to express my thanks to William Walsh, retired federal executive who served the Department of Energy and the National Highway Traffic Safety Administration for many years before becoming an independent automobile safety consultant, who talked to me at length on March 5, 2012. Experience with these agencies is particularly germane to the subject of this book given the highly political nature of highway safety endeavors.

20   Drucker, *Management*, 380.

21   Ibid., 381.

22   Ibid., 381

23   Ibid., 384.

24   Daniel A. Wren, *The History of Management Thought*, 5th ed. (New York: John Wiley & Sons, 2004), 3.

25   Meir Dan-Cohen, "The Value of Ownership," *Journal of Political Philosophy* 9 (2001):404; reprinted in *Harmful Thoughts: Essays on Law, Self, and Morality* by Meir Dan-Cohen (Princeton: Princeton University Press, 2002), 264.

26   Drucker, *Management,* 611.

27   Ibid., 387.

28   Ibid., 395.

29   "Fairness in Firing Teachers," Editorial, *The New York Times*, March 7, 2011, A20.

30   Michael Barbaro, Sharon O'Herman, Javier C. Hernandez, "After 3 Months Mayor Replaces Schools Leader," *The New York Times*, April 3, 2011, A1.

31   Benjamin C. Nelson and Curtis Wood, "Repercussions of Reform: The Effect of Municipal Form of Government on Citizen Participation Strategies," *Journal of Public Administration* 2010-03.

32   Jonathan Weisman, "Democrats Reject Key 9/11 Panel Suggestion," *Washington Post*, November 30, 2006, A1.

33   Richard S. Childs, *The First 50 Years of the Council-Manager Plan of Municipal Government* (New York: National Municipal League, 1965), 1-2.

34   Clarence E. Ridley and Orin F. Nolting, *The City Manager Profession* (Chicago: The University of Chicago Press, 1934), 5.

35   Many local special districts, especially public utilities, also have managerial structures, headed by general managers, chief executive officers, or the equivalent.

36   I had occasion to serve on several panels that interviewed top executives from the City of San Diego who were looking to leave. They explained how the management culture of the organization was being replaced by a political culture, and they wanted out. I have no idea what the political result of abandoning the city manager form of government will be, but it is certain that the city organization will become less and less professional and more and more political.

37   *Practical Lessons from the Loma Prieta Earthquake*, Report from a Symposium Sponsored by the Geotechnical Board and the Board on Natural Disasters of the National Research Council (Washington, DC: National Academy Press, 1994), 1.

38   "Faltering Cancer Trials," *The New York Times*, April 25, 2010, Weekend, 11.

39 Edward Wyatt, "SEC Hurt by Disarray in its Books," *The New York Times*, February 3, 2011, B1.

40 Gene L. Dodaro, "Thirty Steps to Better Government," *The New York Times*, February 16, 2011, A23.

41 Unions have a legal duty to defend and represent employees, and I would not compromise this in any way. Even the most aggressive union representatives know, however, that it is not always in their long-term interest to prevail in the short term.

42 V. Lynn Meek, "Organizational Culture: Origins and Weaknesses," in *Public Sector Management, Theory, Critique and Practice*, ed. David McKevitt and Alan Lawton (Thousand Oaks, CA: SAGE Publications, 1994), 279.

43 Drucker, *Management*, 380-381.

44 David E. Lockwood and George Siehl, *Military Base Closures: A Historical Review from 1988 to 1995*, Congressional Research Service report for Congress, Updated October 18, 2004, found at www.fas.org/sgp/crs/natsec/97-305.pdf, accessed 8/3/12.

45 This publication of the Army Times Publishing Co. is a source of information for senior federal government managers.

46 "Civilian BRAC' could bring major cost savings," *Federal Times*, May 14, 2011, accessed at www.federaltimes.com/article/20110514/ADOP06/105140304/-Civilian-BRAC, 8/7/12.

47   In fact, it is perfectly absurd to think that pay packages worth tens of millions of dollars are necessary to attract capable managers. I have never understood why any owner would employ anyone who demands such extravagance, especially when the demand is for compensation unrelated to results. Baseball's sabermetricians have long since figured out how to calculate players' contributions to wins and losses, though team owners often choose to pay more than is warranted. Surely the private sector can figure out how to pay in accordance with actual contributions.

48   Lockyer v. Andrade, 538 U.S. 63 (2003) No. 01-1127.

49   A generation ago the private sector had both owners and managers. The distinctions were clear, and the portrait of our family example was a valid illustration. Since then, owners have largely disappeared from the private sector, having been replaced by investors. Managers have filled the void created by the departed owners. In doing so, managers left behind not only their long-term, professional, and subordinate perspective, but also the deference, moderation, restraint, caution, and worry that are the manager's portfolio. These were replaced with aggressive and short-term perspectives that owners are free to adopt but managers are not. In many instances the private sector has lost both its owners and its managers. The fact of the matter is that there is a profound absence of managerial values in many parts of the private sector. I have no idea what to do about that, other than to point it out.

50   Timur Kuran, *The Long Divergence: How Islamic Law Held Back the Middle East* (Princeton: Princeton University Press, 2011).

51   Daron Acemoglu and James A. Robinson, *Why Nations Fail* (New York, Crown, 2012), Kindle edition, Section 7665-74.

52   Drucker, *Age of Discontinuity*, 192.

53   Ibid., 193.

Economic Territory

We have noted that aspiring private sector managers attend graduate schools of business, while aspiring public sector managers attend graduate schools of public administration. Those planning careers in the nonprofit sector are free to choose either of those approaches, though an increasing number of programs can be found specializing in the management of nonprofit entities. We take these distinctions for granted, living as we do in a world of business, nonprofit, and government institutions.

We have also noted that all but the tiniest institutions require management to organize, oversee, and ensure that priorities are set and purposes served. One need not be a sophisticated observer to see that institutions of all sorts are much the same around the world. Their purposes vary, but the ways in which people organize and perform do not. One organization chart and structure is pretty much the same as another. All organizations declare goals and means to achieve them. They seek to obtain results commensurate with their resources and capabilities. They employ people to perform myriad functions, few of which are unique. They enter into contracts for goods and services. They have customers. They have plant and equipment. Most important, they seek to improve their financial positions, because financial success is a prerequisite for every other kind of success.

The Top Universal Priority of Organizations

It goes without saying that financial success is essential in business. But it is no less essential to nonprofit and government entities. Each sector has its own distinct language of financial success, but the underlying reality is the same. Financial well-being is the top priority of every institution in existence. Those that are in financial trouble seek to overcome it. Those that are getting by seek to flourish. And those that are flourishing seek to continue to flourish. All institutions evaluate themselves, and measure and report on their standing and progress, in those respects.

Accordingly, top managers everywhere attend to the financial success of the institutions they work for as their highest priority. No one needs to tell them to do this. It is a given. This given may be no more than a manifestation of institutional and managerial self-interest, but more likely it is the organizational equivalent of the biological imperative to replicate. Organizations in strong financial positions cannot be guaranteed future success, but they are more likely to find it than their financially weaker counterparts. In any event, it is a universal truth that whether formally and explicitly called upon to do so or not, top management pursues and values organizational financial success above all other things. This is buried deep in the nature of people and organizations.

There is another factor at work too. It is that organizations can no more maintain the status quo than individuals can stay the same age. Every day things change. Some things go well and others go badly, challenges present themselves, disorder succeeds order, plant and equipment age, and so on. As a result, economic value increases or decreases. When increases are noted, the effects are immediate and positive; when decreases are noted, the effects are immediate and adverse. This makes the practice of management an up and down endeavor. When an organization's economic value rises, management derives satisfaction; when it declines, management must arrest the decline.

Owners, boards of directors, and governing bodies enjoy the prerogative, should they so choose, to direct top management to disregard organizational financial success and pursue some other priority instead. Everywhere and always management would react with incomprehension to such directions. Management would comply, but not comprehend. Simply holding a top management position invests holders with the universal highest value, which is not (for them) susceptible to alteration or replacement. The top managers of business, nonprofit, and government entities, then, have the same top priority.

The Second Universal Priority of Organizations

It may seem peculiar, but organizations are actually created to serve their second priorities, since their first priority is an inescapable given. Second priorities (and lesser ones too) are the ends we typically care about and focus on. And, all things being equal, this is where one would think diversity of purposes and methods come into play. In fact, in a larger sense business, nonprofit, and government organizations share the same second priority as well. It is to add economic value *outside* of their institutional boundaries. Businesses pursue added economic value for the benefit of their owners. Nonprofit entities are focused on and seek to add economic value for the benefit of their clients and the sectors their clients represent, such as the arts, education, environment and animals, health, religion, and a wide range of human services at home and abroad. Agencies and departments of government seek to add economic value for constituents and clients in the sectors where they function.

Consider how success is measured. As we have noted, the key business sector measurement is return on investment or profit. Simply put, this is the amount of money that constitutes economic value added for owners. Businesses exist for the purpose of producing added economic value that can be reinvested or returned to owners at their discretion. If we look at the nonprofit sector, we see why these institutions are thought to be so unlike businesses. Nonprofit institutions are *prohibited from* distributing surplus money to those in control of the organization.[1] Seen more broadly, this is hardly a distinction in kind; it is merely a detail. In fact, the measurements used in the nonprofit sector confirm the central importance of economic value added. Individual nonprofits, and the sector as a whole, track revenues as the key indicator of success. But revenues do not stand alone. Costs must be, and are, tracked in tandem, as are assets. Considered together, these figures paint clear pictures of economic value added (or subtracted), which is exactly what they are supposed to do.[2] These means of measurement, and that which is measured, differ very little from the business sector.

Many will find it easier to accept that business and nonprofit institutions seek to add economic value than to accept that institutions of government do the same. Once again the political nature of government institutions obscures our understanding. The proposition requires development.

Institutions of Government Pursue
Added Economic Value Too

The pursuit of added economic value by institutions of government is recent. It is a product of the Industrial Revolution, which began in England around 1770, and is "still in full flood today." The Industrial Revolution constituted a "drastic break" in the course of history.[3] Among other monumental changes, food became available at affordable prices and life expectancy doubled, from 30 to 60. "Instead of scarcity there was a surplus, instead of marginal subsistence there was amenity."[4]

Before the Industrial Revolution there was little notion of progress. Continuation of the status quo was the best anyone could expect; indeed, change was much more to be feared than welcomed. The swift and thoroughgoing changes brought by the Industrial Revolution taught people to expect things to become different and better. Governments could not but heed these new circumstances. No longer was the well-being of the government the only thing that mattered: the well-being of the population started to matter too.

The Industrial Revolution also ushered in our contemporary world of organizations. As new sources of energy, means of transportation, and communication technologies developed, old organizations were forced to change and new ones were established. The variety, complexity, and success of organizations around the world reflect to a large degree the reach of the Industrial Revolution.

It remains true, of course, that institutions of government are established by political authorities to meet political, not economic, demands. It also remains true that political priorities supersede economic priorities. But everywhere it took hold, the Industrial Revolution brought economic issues to the political stage, often to the front and center. It also brought the ideas of the Enlightenment and other challenges. Myriad volumes have been written on these subjects. For our purposes, it is only necessary to observe that the broad trend line of the past two centuries is one of economic issues looming ever larger.

As a practical matter, this means two things for contemporary politicians. The first is that macroeconomic circumstances always, and microeconomic ones sometimes, impact elections. The second is that individual economic entities—and entire industries around the world—have become political forces to be reckoned with. Despite this, however, economic issues are never the only ones. In good economic times especially, economic issues recede and others move to the forefront. Economic issues are not intrinsically or necessarily political. They are, instead, political to varying degrees reflective of circumstances. On the other hand, economic issues are always of managerial concern. Managers cannot be about the economic well-being of the organizations they serve without also being about those organizations' connections to the larger economy. This is the very nature of the management focus, independent of the focus of political owners at any given time.

As of this writing, three forces are at work pressing institutions of government throughout the developed world to add economic value. First, elected officials are demanding this result, reflecting the economic circumstances of our time. This political demand is at a fever pitch in many places, including the United States, and seems likely to intensify rather than abate. Second, macroeconomic forces are everywhere compelling government institutions to perform better with less money. Even if politicians were not making this demand, the larger economy would be. These cycles tend to come and go, but the current cycle looks to have ushered in a new, and quite possibly long-term, condition. Very few government institutions have avoided the consequences of the recession of 2007, which many think would be better designated as a depression. Government managers did not need politicians to tell them that economic reality had changed, that the ways of the past would no longer serve. Third, there is a value-adding dynamic at work in every institution that has professional management, even if it is weak, as government's management is designed to be. That dynamic is one of management engaged in a permanent quest for better outcomes through improved performance. We have seen that this is what management is about, and that added economic value is the result. It is universally inherent in management that performance is measured in economic terms: there is no other way to measure it. Every government institution, then, to a greater or lesser degree, is subject to management's value-adding contributions.

I recognize that, in the face of the contemporary onslaught of complaints about government being intrinsically wealth-destroying rather than wealth-producing, these arguments may seem theoretical and unpersuasive. A closer look at costs and results is in order.

The Cost of Government

All economic activities have both gross costs and net results. It is curious, but when it comes to government we focus almost exclusively on gross spending and rarely contemplate net results. When we calculate personal net worth or the performance of business or nonprofit institutions, on the other hand, we pass over gross spending and go straight to net results. At the outset, our everyday approach to measuring economic activity reflects positively on individuals, businesses, and nonprofits and negatively on government, before a single bit of data is considered. No doubt there are many reasons for our gross-spending focus in terms of government. It must be granted that we don't know how to measure government's net results. But we don't know how to measure the macroeconomic net results of business or nonprofit activities either.

There is another barrier too, which is that we don't know how to think about, much less measure, the economic well-being of countries. We use GDP numbers in a host of ways to serve that purpose, but no one thinks they tell a complete story. (There aren't too many things economists across the political spectrum agree on, but they do agree that economics is without an accepted measure for the economic well-being of countries.) The very subject of the economic well-being of countries is politically tendentious. It isn't something politically neutral economists spend much time on.

Such attempts as have been made to assess the economic well-being of countries necessarily focus on big-picture summary data that is hard to connect to the enormous universe of detailed data. At the simplistic end of the spectrum we have the "misery index," invented by economist Arthur Okun in the 1960s. It is no more than the sum of the unemployment rate and inflation.[5] There are more sophisticated approaches too, such as the one taken by economists Lars Osberg and Andrew Sharpe in assessing the economic well-being of selected Organization for Economic Cooperation and Development countries (the U.S., U.K., Canada, Australia, Norway, and Sweden) for the period 1980 to 1999. For their study they developed an "Index of Economic Well-being" based on four components: consumption, accumulation, income distribution, and economic security.[6] Yet another approach was taken by the United Nations in its "Inclusive Wealth Report 2012," which measured country wealth in terms of three types of assets: physical capital, including machinery, building, and infrastructure; human capital, including the population's education and skills; and natural capital, including land, forests, fossil fuels, and minerals.[7] We will surely see future approaches that include all of the above and more. Even if we were to reach common agreement on a formula for defining a country's economic well-being, we still lack the means of measuring government's contributions to those outcomes. Nor do we know how to measure the respective contributions of the business or nonprofit sectors.

Economists who attend to big-picture issues tend instead to emphasize macroeconomic theory, especially in regards to the role of central banks, debt, and issues such as stimulus vs. austerity. It is hard to fault them, because these areas are of enormous consequence. Economists also focus on economic behavior. The underlying, axiomatic assumption brought to the study of economic behavior used to be that people and organizations are rational economic actors. This notion is being reassessed, and the discipline of economics is busily attending to this reassessment.

When economists do study the gross and net costs of government activities, it is almost always on a small scale. There is a good and simple reason for this: it is much easier to link assumptions and conclusions to data on a small than a large scale. Even so, economists and policy analysts who perform such studies realize the difficulties inherent in reaching useful conclusions: there is always evidence that can be marshaled in objection to any conclusion. The most common scale of such efforts is exemplified by studies of the costs and benefits of drug courts, at a local or regional level, to determine if the savings achieved in the rest of the criminal justice system offset the cost of the drug courts. (Mostly, but not always, studies conclude that drug courts are cost-effective.) Studies of this nature and at this scale can be found with respect to a great many programs and activities.

Sadly, since no one poses or answers such questions on a large scale, the best we can do is *think about* the large scale economic impacts of government spending. The discipline of economics is not, of course, without terms to use in this regard. The most common terms used by economists in this area are "contributions," "impacts," and "benefits." The term that probably comes closest to what we are looking for is "economic impact," because its general use implies a focus on "net changes in economic activity associated with activities, events, or policies, typically in a given region."[8]

In the absence of a better approach, I propose that we think through the results of government spending in the same way we think through the results of personal or business sector spending. That is, we ask how government spending adds to or subtracts from our country's net worth in the same way we ask how an individual's spending affects his or her net worth or how a business's spending affects its net worth. It may not be a perfect approach, but it will serve our broad conceptual purpose.

What follows is conceptual in nature. I will cite various measurements used by economists to report their findings, but only for the purpose of painting the big picture in terms of the net cost of government. The larger economy defies consistent, rigorous analysis; it is too complex. Readers versed in economic analysis may complain that I am comparing things that are not comparable and mixing and matching data that shouldn't be mixed and matched. So let me stipulate at the outset that what follows is not a contribution to the discipline of economics. It is only a thought exercise and, as such, is intended to ask rather than answer questions.

(Let me also add a personal caveat. I have always loathed the use of the word "investment" when it is applied to government spending. Government does not make investments. It performs functions, each of which has gross costs and net outcomes. Some government expenditures add to our country's economic net worth; others subtract from it. The cost of government in the end is the total of these net figures. Let me hasten to add as well that economic values are not everything; they are just the subject at hand.)

Perhaps the best way to show how this works is through a personal example. My wife and I bought our first home in 1971. We have made mortgage payments, reroofed, and incurred other costs of homeownership over the years, but in the end owning our home, despite the recent decline in real estate values, has added to our net worth. Home ownership for us has been better than free—it has been an economic positive. The cost of tuition for our children is another set of expenditures that has worked the same way: over the long term the tuition payments we made will add to, rather than subtract from, our family's net worth. In these examples there was a prerequisite: we had to be able to afford the expenditures in order to enjoy the benefits. But we didn't intend either our housing or education spending as investments. We bought our home to live in, and paid for our children's education because they desired it and we valued it. The other set of costs that falls into this category is health care. Some of those costs could have been avoided without adverse economic effect, but others—emergency surgeries and care for long-term conditions—have been essential to life and limb. I can't think of any other categories of spending that, as a whole, served our family's net worth in the same way as housing, education, and health care, although numerous other individual expenses served the purpose too, such as transportation costs to go to work. We have also engaged in spending that contributed to our happiness but decreased our net worth, although it served to increase the net worth of others. In exactly the same way, government spending produces a variety of results in terms of our country's net worth and economic well-being.

The concept is simple: the net result of every economic activity is the sum total of its economic plusses and minuses. If all those plusses and minuses were discoverable, we could readily calculate our country's economic net worth.

(This would not be the same thing as economic well-being, but that is another discussion. See below.) Every economic activity would be seen to add some amount to the country's net worth or subtract a different amount from it. It may be an advantage to this thought exercise that we don't know how to turn the concept into actual equations, since the acceptability of the concept would immediately become dependent on the conclusions it produced.

Before moving on to the cost of government functions, perhaps it would be instructive to apply the approach to some nongovernmental examples. My objective is not to laud or denigrate any of the selected economic activities, but to set forth the concept in familiar terms. Consider the computer industry, an innovative and expanding engine of growth that has contributed greatly to prosperity and productivity advances around the world. Positive aspects include the immense amount of economic activity associated with the industry and productivity improvements across the economy. But the computer industry has economic negatives as well, including rare earth materials depletion, fossil fuel consumption, pollution, various health costs, and perhaps even the economic cost of behavioral changes associated with computer use. No doubt whatever is added to our country's net worth by the computer industry is far greater than what is subtracted, but the fact remains that the industry generates both additions and subtractions. Then there is the auto industry, which generates economic activity in abundance and provides jobs around the world. It has negatives too, including the costs of resource depletion, pollution, injuries and deaths associated with auto accidents, and so on. These examples are no more than back-of-the-envelope observations. At best they illustrate the outer layer, if you will, of the concept. We know for sure that economic activities produce net economic results. We just don't know how to identify and measure them all. They are almost certainly discoverable, however, even if we don't know how to derive them at present. Let us, then, apply the concept to the major functions of government.

Costs by Function

Consider the net cost of government spending for transportation, including streets, highways, bridges, ports, rail, airports, and so on. This is the classic example of government as a contributor to economic well-being. Supporters of transportation spending proposals always call that spending "investment." Early in our country's history there was vigorous debate about whether or not government should build roads and canals, and the question was answered that it should. About 5% of total annual government spending today goes to transportation—on average 1.7% of GDP— while the transportation sector constitutes 11% of GDP. No one knows the exact net cost of government transportation spending. The sector as a whole has long been thought to be economically efficacious. Every project and each increment of spending has its own plusses and minuses, adding some amount to and subtracting a different amount from the country's net worth.

Government spending on clean water, sewage treatment, and trash collection and disposal are further examples of activities widely seen as economically efficacious. The economic costs of not having clean drinking water, sewer systems, and trash collection and disposal would arguably be hugely greater than the costs of having them. And it would make no economic sense for individuals, neighborhoods, businesses, and so on to provide those goods for themselves.

The same is true for the "protection" category of government spending, which includes police and fire. We almost never contemplate the economic value of these services. But we see small examples of economic value every day and big ones from time to time. The 1969 police and fire strike in sedate Toronto, Canada, was cited in the Introduction as a classic example of what happens in the absence of government authority (in that instance, sixteen hours of mayhem and arson). Cities in bankruptcy are demonstrating the point in 2012. In Stockton, California, residents report that the police force has been reduced to responding only when there is blood. Spending on private security and other measures has soared.[9] This scenario is played out every time a city in bankruptcy slashes police services. It seems highly probable that cutting spending on police beyond a given threshold is a net economic negative. Nor can private security make up for deficiencies in police services, because private security depends on government backup, from police and fire to courts and jails and more.

All of these functions together constitute a little over 10% of total government spending. My long experience at the local level tells me that many people regard these as examples of government at its economic best. Everyone is connected to these government services; their indispensability is intuitive. Over nearly forty years in local government I almost never heard any complaints about the cost of these functions. Indeed, I was on the receiving end of a perpetual demand for more of them. We do not know the net cost of these functions, but my experience tells me that these functions constitute net positives. They may well be very substantial positives.

Now, let's contemplate public education, which constitutes about 15% of total government spending. So far as I can determine, few have ventured to assess the macroeconomic outcomes associated with this huge sector of the economy, and no wonder; it would be a hugely complex proposition. Not knowing how, I do not propose to fill this void. Still, we can think about the big picture in instructive economic terms. There are two obvious approaches to assessing the net cost of public education. The first is to assess each of the many components and add them all up. The second is to see what those who avail themselves of private education pay, and then make correlations. Each would be a monumental endeavor in its own right, but overviews can be readily offered.

Education confers economic benefit primarily through contributions to employment and economic growth. For individuals and societies there is a strong correlation between employment, which generates income, and education. Greater educational attainments serve to increase personal income and overall economic growth. Although the exact relationship is unknown, education and economic growth are clearly complementary.[10] It also appears that educational attainment correlates with lower social costs, such as welfare and other assistance programs. Those with more education also tend to be healthier and commit fewer crimes.[11] Cause and effect in such regards, of course, is hard to pin down.

Turning to the second broad approach, the economic value of education is evidenced by how much individuals are willing to pay for private education, from preschool to graduate school. Although the sums paid to private schools may not be 100% reflective of economic values, the marketplace clearly places a high value on education. Further marketplace evidence can be seen in the home values of similar homes in school districts of different quality. Home buyers everywhere pay a premium to be in the best school districts.

Higher education has long been thought to be essential to economic growth and well-being. Two recent studies typical of the genre offer numbers in addition to concepts for consideration. For readers who want more, the classic—and most scholarly—overview may be *The Economic Value of Higher Education,* a publication of the American Council on Education/Macmillan Series on Higher Education written in 1988.[12]

The first study, titled *The Value of Higher Education: Individual and Societal Benefits (With Special Consideration for the State of Arizona)* was published in 2005. It was done as part of a larger research project called the *Productivity and Prosperity Project (P3)* and conducted by the L. William Seidman Research Institute in the W.P. Carey School of Business at Arizona State University. The purpose of the project was to "inform debate on a broad set of issues related to achieving economic prosperity for all citizens of Arizona."[13]

Three professional economists authored the study. I am in no position to argue whether their results are more or less authoritative than any other results, but the results are typical of professional economic work on the subject. In terms of private economic benefit, the authors' first conclusion (of nine) is, as might be expected, that individual earnings correlate strongly to educational attainment. In terms of societal benefits, the first outcome cited (of eight) is that greater educational attainments contribute to "enhanced worker productivity" which in turn translates into "higher output and incomes for the economy."[14] The authors go on to review national and Arizona-specific data as well as scholarly work by others in the effort to quantify the larger benefits of higher education spending. They suggest that the societal value of a bachelor's degree in the U.S. in 2002-03 represented a return of 15.7% for men and 16.6% for women.[15] In other words, "Higher education represents an economic investment with a very high return—almost twice the size of long-run returns on stocks."[16]

In a similar but less comprehensive study published in 2011, Dave Swenson of Iowa State University concluded that for every dollar spent providing higher education at Iowa's public universities an additional $.78 in industrial output was added. The economic value added by each dollar spent on Iowa's community colleges was estimated to be $.74.[17]

The net economic impact of public education spending in terms of the country's net worth is no doubt discoverable, but discovering it would be far more challenging than deriving the net costs of transportation or protection. It seems reasonable to suppose that a poorly performing education sector could constitute a substantial negative in terms of the country's net worth. On the other hand, it also seems reasonable to think that a by and large competent public education sector would serve to increase the country's net worth in the same way my family's education spending contributed to my family's net worth.

Thought exercises such as those in the preceding examples could readily be undertaken with respect to every government function. In each case the plusses and minuses associated with the activity must be set forth and added up. Most functions of government include multiple positives to be added into the net worth equation. But there are two big categories where this process alone would be incomplete: defense spending and transfer payments.

Defense spending is arguably the exception to my assertion that the net cost of government is discoverable. At best we have an imperfect understanding of the gross costs and results of defense choices made. Net costs are another matter altogether. To derive them we would have to know how things would have turned out if we had made different defense choices. Still, there are some useful things we can say in terms of the domestic economic impacts of defense spending.

Robert Barro and Charles Redlick studied defense spending from 1914 to 2006 and concluded that during normal economic times the multiplier from defense spending for the domestic economy is about .67, but that when the economy is weak it rises by .05 for each percentage point by which unemployment exceeds 5.6%. In other words, about two-thirds of what is spent for defense in normal times does not subtract from the country's net worth.[18] This is very good news, because defense spending is not generally thought of as economically efficacious, the goal of the defense enterprise being *not* to put its products to use. In addition, it must be noted that defense spending has produced numerous technological advances that have been shared with the larger economy, and contributed to the country's net worth in areas such as jet engines, GPS systems, and the

Internet. We don't need to conjure alternative histories to find positive contributions from defense spending. But we can't quantify them either.

In terms of alternative histories, Robert Kagan makes the case for a net positive result for defense spending. He argues that the "enormous benefits this strategy [the U.S.'s post-World War II defense policy] has provided, including the financial benefits, somehow never appear on the ledger." Kagan argues that U.S. defense spending and policy is essential to "the prevention of major war, the support of an open trading system, and promotion of the liberal principles of free markets and free government. How much is that order worth? What would be the cost of its collapse or transformation into another type of order?"[19] I hope Mr. Kagan is correct, given that his larger world view is by and large shared by both political parties. In any event, the questions he has posed are entirely appropriate, and they should be posed about other sets of expenditures too.

Let us now turn to the last category of government spending we will consider, which is transfer payments. Simply put, transfer payments are government-directed redistributions of income. The biggest such economic activity is Social Security, which transfers income from wage earners to retirees. Other examples are pensions, unemployment insurance, food stamps, welfare, a variety of assistance programs, and subsidies of all sorts, including tax expenditures. These costs are second only to those of the health care sector in their economic importance and impact. (Medicare, Medicaid, and other health care activities are also transfer programs, but they are generally dealt with separately and in their own right, which we will do below.)

The net worth question for each of these programs is essentially about the respective uses to which taxpayers would have put the money if they had not been taxed compared to the uses of those to whom the money was transferred. (The administrative costs of each transfer program must also be factored in.) Lowell Gallaway and Richard Vedder argue that the cost of transfer payments in the U.S. for most of the 1990s reduced "real per capita levels of output to levels that are about one-eighth below what they might have been." That is, "the greater part of that portion of the higher incomes which is taxed away would have been used for the accumulation of additional capital. Without that capital, economic growth slows."[20] Gallaway and Vedder's work suggests that the multiplier figure per dollar of transfer tax is .62. They also cite "one of the more notable works" on the subject that sets forth a multiplier range of between .50 and .80 for transfer taxes as a whole.[21] In this view, the economic efficacy of transfer taxes may be worse than or about the same as defense spending (as seen by Barrow and Redlick). Mary Keegan Eamon of the University of Illinois, on the other hand, argues that transfer programs "have been linked by numerous researchers to increases in state and/or local tax revenue and economic activity. Increased consumer spending and economic activity from receipt of public benefits positively affect employment, increase earnings and enhance property values, even in more affluent neighborhoods, indirectly benefitting non-recipients."[22]

The longstanding transfer programs of the sort noted above have long been and are likely to remain manageable. That is not the case for the prospective economic impacts of state and local pension costs. It is widely recognized that the long-term benefits promised to state and local employees and retirees cannot possibly be paid. For better or worse, the salient aspect of unfunded liabilities in state and local pension systems is largely overlooked. It is this: benefits that cannot be paid will not be paid. Regardless of their legal obligations to do so, retirement systems will not send checks to retirees with money they do not have. Sooner or later, one retirement system at a time, economic reality will dictate outcomes where politically and economically workable solutions have not already been put in place. There will be no "bailouts." For this reason, unfunded pension liabilities will not turn out to be the disaster many forecast for state and local governments: the disaster will be for their retirees instead. The same is true for unfunded retiree health care benefits. (Given this, it is curious that supporters of pension and retiree health care benefits so often oppose reforms that would render reduced benefits viable; one would think that, from their point of view, benefit reform would be preferable to benefit dissolution.)

I have saved health care, the most difficult and most consequential subject, for last. Health care is the largest and fastest growing sector of the economy, as well as the largest and fastest growing component of government spending. Health care spending in 2011 was about $2.5 trillion, constituting about 18% of the U.S. economy. The economic efficaciousness of this spending is of vital importance. One by one, each component of the health care sector adds to or subtracts from country net worth by some unknown amount. If we intend to do anything about the rising costs of health care, we need to know what those amounts are and what might be done to improve net economic outcomes.

At the broadest conceptual level, it is clear that improved health is an economic positive. John Lechleiter, CEO and Chairman of Eli Lilly & Co., has argued that increased life expectancy—from 39 in 1960 to 67 in 1990—has been the single biggest contributor to economic growth in Asia.[23] Improvements in health contribute to increased labor market productivity, wages, and overall employment, as well as to a growing health care sector that provides employment, innovation, and capital formation. On the other hand, Dr. Donald Berwick, former Director of the Center for Medicare and Medicaid Services, estimates that between 20% and 30% of total U.S. health care expenditures—perhaps $1 trillion per year—produce no benefits for patients.[24] If it is true that this much is being spent unproductively, it must also be true that many other productive activities are being crowded out across the economy.

Economists' chief concern about health care spending is the rate of growth, which seems bound to affect every sector of the economy. The United States is an "outlier" country in terms of health care spending; we spend a great deal more than most countries and don't appear to derive benefit from doing so. The majority point of view among economists is that continued rapid growth in health care spending will lower overall economic growth and employment. The minority point of view is that increases in health spending are at worst neutral for the larger economy and might even be positive if they result in better health and improved productivity.[25]

Health care spending generates positive or negative outcomes through the following mechanisms. On the positive side, the U.S. Department of Health and Human Services (HHS) cites two macroeconomic plusses: 1) health care spending produces better health and higher labor market productivity, which leads to increased wages and overall employment, and 2) health care spending produces increased incomes and employment in the health care and related sectors. On the negative side, HHS cites five factors: 1) employers offset increased health care costs with reduced investment, increased prices, and lower employment, 2) higher taxes for health spending reduce individuals' after-tax incomes, 3) increased borrowing by the federal government for health spending fuels inflation, 4) government entities reduce spending on infrastructure and education in favor of health care, and 5) increased health care spending reduces what consumers can spend on other things.[26]

In sum, the available evidence suggests that "health care costs can have both a positive and a negative impact on the economy."[27] One of the reasons it evades determination is that as per capita income rises people spend more on health care, which establishes a correlation between increased income and increased health care spending. But the positive relationship between increased health care spending and increased per capita income "does not rule out the possibility that health care cost growth has a [net] negative effect on the economy."[28]

What is the net cost of health care at present? What will it be in the future? No one knows. It seems self-evident that health care for the economically productive and those who will be economically productive in the future is more economically efficacious than health care for the retired. (One can imagine the consequences for any politician who would say such a thing!) But retirees participate in the economy, making contributions to country net worth that to some degree serve to offset health care transfer costs. That is about as much as anyone can definitively say. Health care promises to be the consuming political and economic issue of the future. One of our highest priorities as a society must be to discover and respond to the actual economic results of health care spending.

Government Spending and the Country's Net Worth

Volumes would be required to do justice to all the functions discussed above. At best, an inconclusive sampling has been offered. The point of the sampling is not to say what conclusions should be reached about the economic results of any given function of government, but what considerations should be brought to bear in the process of reaching conclusions.

If one were to laboriously review the hundreds of kinds of economic activities that take place in our country, the economic superiority of those in the private sector compared to those in the public sector would not be evident. Consider just a few examples. If shopping centers are economic positives, the roads and public utilities that serve them cannot be economic negatives. If private schools are positives, public ones cannot inherently be negatives. If private homes and apartments are positives, police and fire services cannot be negatives. If private hospitals are positives, public ones cannot be inherently negative. If making an environmental mess is a positive, cleaning it up cannot be a negative. Page after page of similar examples could be offered. It is not possible to conceive of the country's net worth absent the economic contributions of government. Nor is there anything about the everyday functions of government that distinguish them from everyday private sector activities in terms of economic worth.

It would be silly to think that the public sector can generate prosperity and growth as well as the private sector. I am arguing no such thing. The private sector is inherently superior in those regards, for a multitude of reasons. Simply put, the private sector places economic values first, while the public sector places political values first. The private sector is also assertively managed, while the public sector ranges from not managed at all to "management lite." To acknowledge the desirability of a robust private sector, however, does not oblige one to denigrate the economic value of the public sector.

Let us think about the country's net worth in terms of the three categories of government spending noted in the previous section. The first covers the basic "functions" of government, the second category national defense, and the third transfer payments.

Government spending for what I have referred to as "functions" adds to the country's net worth and economic well-being in exactly the same way that my family's spending on housing, education, and health care has added to our family's net worth and economic well-being. If all that spending could somehow be erased from our country's history, we would be a poorer rather than a richer country. The functions are indispensable, which is why government provides them. In fact, the economic cost of the absence of each function would exceed the cost of its provision.

The economic returns on basic government functions

are steady but modest. This is not where we look for higher-level contributions to the country's net worth. Many government programs, however, do produce rather handsome returns. The results of public health programs, food safety standards, auto safety measures, weather forecasting, flood control, and hundreds of other such programs can be quite substantial. To cite a recent example, New Orleans has a new $15 billion hurricane protection system. If there are no hurricanes over the useful life of these improvements, that spending will have been mostly a net negative. But if there are many such storms, the project will constitute a large positive. The odds are high that the economic benefits of these improvements will be substantial.

The public sector has also produced outsized economic positives in the past and will do so in the future. Government-supported academic research has long been thought of as the premier wealth producer for the future. If the human genome project, to cite just one example, leads to breakthrough medical advances, research done in public universities will have been the impetus. Government agencies themselves sometimes produce outsized economic benefits too. Consider the burgeoning industry for hydraulic fracturing of natural gas. For thirty years the federal Department of Energy contributed to this activity's development through laboratory research, microseismic GPS mapping, partnerships with private companies, the funding of experiments in underground explosives that were too expensive and risky for private investors to undertake, and the like.[29] It is impossible to say what the added economic value of this new industry might be for our country. Whatever that value turns out to be, the federal government will have been integral to its development.

On a much larger scale, the World Bank estimates that the cost of a severe influenza pandemic could cost the world economy $3 trillion.[30] The prevention of such a pandemic by public health authorities would surely qualify as a positive on every country's ledger. If and when the avoidance of such a pandemic can be demonstrated, public health authorities will have made a rather astoundingly large contribution to economic worth.

In sum, the public sector engages in a substantial number and wide range of functions that bear on economic growth and prosperity and deserve a place in those ledgers. This is why across-the-board cuts in government spending—austerity measures, if you will—are so often economically counterproductive. Increases in government spending can be and often are economic positives, while decreases can be and often are economic negatives. It would make things a lot easier for elected officials if reducing the size of the public sector would, in and of itself, make a country richer. But the world is not that simple.

The contribution to the country's net worth by government spending in the second category, defense, is, as we have seen, more difficult to ascertain. No one can prove one case or another. All we can say for sure is that bipartisan political majorities over the long term have supported our country's defense spending. This is as good an indication of economic worth as can be obtained.

The third category, transfer payments, requires a great deal more in the way of assessment. Unfortunately, the subject is so politically tendentious that neutral economic analysis is almost impossible to come by. Some think that the idea of such transfers is both morally wrong and economically counterproductive. Others think these payments are morally obligatory as well as economically productive. I don't know if there will ever be a way to answer the moral question, but the economic one is answerable. Program by program, transfer payments accomplish economic outcomes that can be measured. How those outcomes affect the country's economic net worth and well-being can also be measured.

In summary, it seems highly probable that, as a whole, government spending for functions is a worthy contributor to the country's net worth. It also seems probable that government spending for defense and transfer payments subtracts from the country's net worth to some degree. Up to now the proportions of spending for these three large purposes have probably not been hugely consequential. Though defense spending may not change much in the years ahead, transfer payments are another matter. As they grow, and they are set to grow rapidly, it seems all but certain that government spending on functions will have to be cut to make room for them. This could in turn adversely affect government's future contributions to the country's net worth. We may be at risk of entering a circle in which we are repeatedly called upon to cut government's most valuable contributions to net worth to make room for government's less economically efficacious activities.

Given increasing health care costs and our aging population, economists have good reason to worry about how these bills will be paid. This is why the net cost of health care matters so much for the larger economy. The impact of health care spending on our country's net worth will be much more about the net cost of health care as a function than about whether those bills are paid privately or by government.

Net Costs and Management

In theory, elected officials and candidates for office should want to know the net costs of government activities as best as they can be determined. Those who want less government should want to know net costs to help them render smaller government more efficacious. Those who want more government should want to know net costs to help them choose among competing needs. Both sets should want to know net costs for their own understanding and to help them shape public opinion. In practice, it is better not to know such things. Evidence that what one supports is an economic negative is inadmissible, as is evidence that what one opposes is actually a positive. Politics is not about economic merit.

As far as the public is concerned, government is about only two kinds of numbers, gross spending and tax rates. While it is true that our knowledge of the rest of the picture is incomplete, that incompleteness is not the cause of our narrow focus. If it were, we would suffer from the same narrow focus in terms of understanding private sector results, and we don't. Whatever the reason(s) may be, we apply an operative world view to government that does not concern itself with net costs and results.

It therefore falls to government career managers to be concerned about net costs—past, present, and future—even though their bosses are not. As a practical matter, government's managers probably know more than anyone else about the costs and benefits of the programs they oversee. They are not economists and they do not produce economic studies. They simply know costs and results. They have a streetwise, rather than academic, view of net costs.

Still, despite the limitations of their knowledge, they are duty-bound to advise their bosses of their views in these regards. Political owners are free to accept, alter, or ignore management's opinions and advice. But politicians should not be free to resist or censor management's information. If career managers don't introduce and promote understanding of net costs, no one will. These costs and results are well within management's purview.

It is even more important that management share its focus on net costs with employees. They are the people who actually produce net results, and whose futures depend to a large degree on economic performance, despite the commonly held view to the contrary. It is in the self-interest of government organizations, then, as well as the public interest, to assess and understand performance in economic terms, even for agencies whose purposes may seem removed from economic matters.

Finally, there is another much larger and *more* important reason that net costs matter. It is this: knowing what things actually cost is a prerequisite for bringing values other than economic ones to bear. We noted at the outset of this discussion that economic values are not and should not be the only values at issue. Economic values are just the easiest to measure. It is entirely appropriate for the public and its elected officials to weigh other values higher than economic values. In the absence of knowing what economic costs actually are, it is difficult if not impossible to weigh the merits of competing, less readily measured values. Knowing more about economic costs is a precondition for bringing other values to the fore. Being principally about economic values, management is in an ideal position to promote economic understanding and at the same time set the stage for elected officials to address other values.

Economic Well-Being

We cannot conclude this review without broadening the picture a bit. Net worth is a means, after all, not an end—it has no intrinsic meaning or importance. Neither individuals nor countries pursue net worth for net worth's sake. What is actually being pursued is economic well-being. Suppose you are taking an economics class and have been assigned to write an equation to express your individual financial well-being. What would that equation look like? What terms would it include, and how would they be weighed? What probabilities would have to be accounted for? How much would luck factor into the equation?

Let me suggest a number of terms, in no particular order, for insertion in the personal economic well-being equation: your individual and family net worth; your education; the economic viability of what you do for a living; the economic well-being of your community, state, and country (and these days the rest of the world too); the economic viability of Social Security and Medicare (for those who depend on those programs); the economic viability of your health care company; the odds of a health care event that exceeds your policy's limits, given that medical costs are the largest cause of personal bankruptcy; the odds of lawsuits, judgments, or other costs that could lead to major losses or bankruptcy; the odds of a natural disaster adverse to your economic well-being; and so on. It doesn't take much contemplation to see that there are risks to individual economic well-being that even high net worth cannot protect against.

Every country's economic well-being is also at the mercy of things beyond its control. If it would be a struggle to write a personal economic well-being equation, imagine how complex the equation for a country would be. Some would say that the concept of economic well-being for both individuals and countries is value-laden, but I would submit otherwise. Economic well-being is material well-being. No doubt people will hold a great variety of opinions about it, as they do about, say, their health. But health, like economic well-being, is measureable, in both particular and overall terms. A person in the healthiest 1% might think his health was average, but he would be wrong. The concept of economic well-being works in the same way. The people of whichever country ranked #1 in economic well-being might or might not feel like #1. Nevertheless, economic well-being, meaning standing in terms of material goods and services, is a material fact, not an opinion.

The concept of economic well-being does not match the breadth or depth of the questions Robert Kagan posed about defense spending. Recall that, reflecting on the net cost of U.S. national defense and related activities to maintain order internationally, he asked, "How much is that order worth?" and "What would be the cost of its collapse or transformation into another type of order?[31] These questions apply to the costs of our domestic order too. There wouldn't be much point in safeguarding international order in the absence of a domestic order worth preserving. Mr. Kagan's questions, then, are the most vital questions of all.

They are also far beyond management. Indeed, they are beyond politics most of the time. They come into play only when the actual order of things is threatened, at which time protection is invariably undertaken without regard to cost. That fact should tell us something about the economic value of government too.

Full Circle

We have observed many times throughout this book that management is first and foremost about money. Accordingly, the total universe of economic matters and concerns is pertinent to management. We have also observed that political values supersede managerial concerns. Regardless of political direction, though, government's management is about adding economic value through organizational performance.

Management's specific economic purpose is twofold: to strengthen the economic standing of the agency served, and to add economic value outside the agency by performing effectively. It would be helpful to know net costs but it is not essential. Management adds economic value by improving the positive net results of functions that add to the country's net worth and by decreasing the net negative results of functions that subtract from net worth. It is not necessary to know every particular in order to achieve both any more than it is necessary for business executives to know their net contributions to the country's net worth.

Our conception of public sector management is grossly distorted by our insistence on seeing the economic contributions of the private and public sectors as different in kind. They are not. The actual difference in kind, as we saw in the

Introduction, is about the sources of these sectors' money. The private sector's money comes from voluntary transactions with customers, while the public sector's money comes from taxation. This is the distinction that matters, because it is the distinction underlying the supremacy of political values in government.

The business sector constitutes a little less than two-thirds of the economy, while government is a little more than a third. Nonprofits are about 5%. The general populace is obliged to engage in the major sectors of economic activity represented by the business sector, but by and large has a wide range of choices in terms of individual institutions to engage with. These institutions are, with a few exceptions, allowed to fail when they cannot earn their way. The institutions of government, on the other hand, are supported through taxation. It is mandatory that everyone pay for them because the political, economic, and social order depends on it. Is it not curious that as a society we recognize that the business sector requires strong and capable management to achieve economic success, but are not willing to even ask ourselves if the organizations of government might have the same need if they are to attain the same result?

Endnotes

1   Richard Steinberg, "Economic Theories of Nonprofit Organizations," in *The Non-Profit Sector: A Research Handbook*, edited by Walter W. Powell and Richard Steinberg, 2nd edition (New Haven: Yale University Press, 2006), 118.

2   See "The Nonprofit Sector in Brief, Public Charities, Giving, and Volunteering, 2011," at www.urgan.org, nonprofit almanac brief 2011 pdf (accessed 6/5/2012).

3   S.E. Finer, *The History of Government*, Volume 3, 1609.

4   Ibid., 1619.

5   See www.miseryindex.us/ (accessed June 11, 2012).

6   Lars Osberg and Andrew Sharpe, *An Index of Economic Well-Being for Selected OECD Countries,* Review of Income and Wealth, Series 48, Number 3, September 2002.

7   Free exchange, "The real wealth of nations," *The Economist*, June 30, 2012, 78. The full UN report is found at "InclusiveWealthReport2012," www.ihdp.unu.edu/article/iwr. This report found that the U.S. is the second wealthiest country in the world, just behind Japan, with a national wealth of $117.8 trillion. *The Economist* article and the UN report, which was overseen by Sir Partha Dasgupta of Cambridge University, acknowledge the fledgling nature of the work and also that "the [economic] profession does not really reward this work."

8   Philip Watson, Joshua Wilson, Dawn Thilmany, and Susan Winter, "Determining Economic Contributions and Impacts: What is the difference and why do we care?" *The*

Journal of Regional Analysis and Policy, Volume 37, Number 2, 2007, 140-146.

9   Malia Woolan, "Years of Unraveling, Then Bankruptcy for a City," *The New York Times*, July 19, 2012, 1.

10   Dana Mitra, "Pennsylvania's Best Investment: The Social and Economic Benefits of Public Education," at www.elc-pa.org/BestInvestment_Full_Report_6.27.11pdf, 9-12.

11   Ibid., 13-21.

12   Larry L. Leslie and Paul T. Brinkman, *The Economic Value of Higher Education,* American Council on Education/Macmillan Series on Higher Education (New York: Macmillan Publishing Co., 1988).

13   Kent Hill, Ph.D., Dennis Hoffman, Ph.D., and Tom R. Rex, MBA, *The Value of Higher Education: Individual and Societal Benefits (With Special Consideration for the State of Arizona),* October 2005, L. William Seidman Research Institute, W.P. Carey School of Business, Arizona State University, Tempe, Arizona, at www.wpcarey.asu.edu/...Value%20Full%20Report_final_october%25200 (accessed 8/16/2012).

14   Ibid., 1.

15   Ibid., 30.

16   Ibid., 55.

17   Dave Swenson, *Measuring the Total Economic Value of State-Funded Higher Education in Iowa,* Department of Economics, Iowa State University, April 2011, at www.econ.iastate.edu/research/other/p122778 (accessed 8/16/2012).

18   Robert J. Barrow and Charles J. Redlick, "Macroeconomic Effects from Government Purchases and Taxes,"
Harvard University, January 2010, at www.economics.mit.
edu/files/5276 (accessed 6/19/2012).

19   Kagan, Robert, "The Price of Power," *The Weekly Standard*, Volume 16, No. 18, at www.weeklystandard.com/ar-
ticles/price-power533696.html (accessed January 24, 2012).

20   Lowell Gallaway and Richard Vedder, "The Impact of
Transfer Payments on Economic Growth: John Stuart Mill
Versus Ludwig Von Mises," *The Quarterly Journal of Aus-
trian Economics*, Vol. 5 No. 1 (Spring 2002) 57-65.

21   Charles L. Ballard, John B. Shoven, and John Whal-
ley, "A General Equilibrium Computation of the Marginal-
Welfare Costs of Taxation in the United States," *American
Economic Review* (March 1985), 128-38.

22   Forrest, Sharita, "Social welfare cuts ultimately come
with heavy price, researchers say," www.news.illinois.edu/
news/12/0523publicbenefitsprogramsMaryEamon.html
(accessed 6/14/2012).

23   Interview with *The Wall Street Journal*, at www.wsj.
com/article/SB10001424052970203611404577042813309
766648.html (accessed 6/20/2012).

24   Interviewatwww.reforminghealth.org/2011/12/14don-
berwick-tell-what-he-really-thinks-about-cms-health-re-
form (accessed 3/15/2012).

25   Neeraj Sood, Arkadipta Ghosh, and Jose J. Escarse, "The
Effect of Health Care Cost Growth on the U.S. Economy,

Final Report," Office of the Assistant Secretary for Planning and Evaluation (ASPE), U.S. Department of Health and Human Services (HHS), September, 2007, 4, at http://aspe.hhs.gov/health/costgrowth/ (accessed 6/21/2012).

26 Ibid., 5.

27 Ibid., 29.

28 Ibid., 29.

29 Michael Shellenberger, Ted Nordhaus, Alex Trembath, and Jesse Jenkins, *Breakthrough Institute research and interviews show the direct and sustained support federal agencies provided to the gas industry leading up to the modern natural gas revolution,* The Breakthrough Institute, at http://thebreakthrough.org/blog/2011/12/newinvestigationfinds-decade.shtml (accessed 7/22/2012). Also see "There's Still Hope for the Planet" by David Leonhardt, *The New York Times,* Sunday Review, July 22, 2012, 1.

30 Jim Robbins, "Man-Made Epidemics," *The New York Times*, Sunday Review, July 15, 2012, 1.

31 Kagan, op cit.

Conclusion
In Pursuit of Larger Purposes

We have seen that elected officials and their political appointees on the one hand, and career executives and managers on the other, are about different things. But suppose we elevate our sights from the practical, everyday demands faced by our subjects to larger purposes. Aren't these two groups both about achieving better government? And isn't that a goal not divisible into political and managerial aspects?

The answer is that politicians and management are not about the same larger purpose or purposes. In the noblest sense, politicians are about the aspirations of society and the role of government in the achievement of those aspirations. In election after election, politicians offer their take on the matters of greatest concern to voters, and the voters decide who will govern. Given the impossibly large number of issues in play at any given time, and the complexities involved in all of them, clear directions from voters are very hard, if not impossible, to come by. Arguably elections are more about *who* will govern than *how* they will govern. But this need not be thought of as problematic. David Deutsch argues that, by submitting alternative choices to voters, democracies advance knowledge about how to achieve a better society.[1] This does not mean that every candidate and election serves that purpose, but it does mean that over time a society open to change and improvement can judge for itself how to proceed.

Most societies through human history have been what Deutsch calls "static" societies. They apply their people's creativity to the maintenance of stasis. This is a nasty phenomenon; static societies, as Deutsch says, were and are miserable places. Democracies, on the other hand, employ human creativity to advance knowledge for the purpose of making better lives. Politicians are at the forefront of creating societal knowledge. They are at the forefront of creating better lives when they are right about things, and creating worse ones when they are wrong. Politicians are correct when they say that the stakes of the next election—and every election—are high.

Career executives and managers also have a noble calling, but it is orders of magnitude less grand than that of their political masters. Management's larger purpose is to advance knowledge of a narrower and different sort: knowledge about the public's institutions. These institutions can accomplish many things, but there are also many things beyond their reach. Absent management's knowledge and experience, political owners cannot factor institutional realities into their political equations.

In its everyday work, then, management applies what it knows to the operation of public organizations. In pursuit of its larger purpose, management shares what it knows with the elected officials it works for and, to the greatest extent possible, with the public the elected officials work for. Management does not *report to* the public, but promotes public understanding by citing issues faced, choices made, costs contemplated and incurred, successes achieved, and failures suffered. Management is mostly comfortable doing this one institution at a time, but must stretch to address government in its entirety. The way to obtain performance, then, which is management's essential top priority, is to promote and expand knowledge and experience related to institutions and the outcomes they produce.

Elected officials and their representatives will always be free to accept, reject, or modify the recommendations of management. Managerial values will never be controlling. But they must be there for owners to consider, whether the owners want to consider them or not. Management cannot be absolved of the responsibility to recommend. The political owners of the institutions of government must be in receipt of everything management has to offer.

Government career managers have been silenced because their values are rightly subordinate to political values. But this silencing is a terrible mistake for public institutions. Career executives and managers must speak. They have much to say. It is a given that their focus is narrow and that they are subordinate to their elected bosses. But instead of serving as an impediment, this fundamental reality should free management to speak. Correctly understood, managerial speech does not infringe on political authority or political prerogatives; it supplements that authority and those prerogatives instead.

The institutions of government matter. When they fail, it is next to impossible for anything else to succeed. When they succeed, abundant opportunities emerge for all sorts of other things to succeed. The fact is that public institutions are not necessary evils, as they are often portrayed in today's political climate, but indispensable assets. They require strong and capable political leadership. They require strong and capable management too.

In short, a theory of public administration for our time must *not* be a theory of politics. Peter Drucker wrote that, "Ultimately we will need political theories appropriate to the realities and needs of the society of organizations."[2] There may or may not ever be such a political theory. For our more narrow purposes, though, it is clear that a theory of public administration must be a robust theory of performance-oriented management. It must address how to identify and replicate organizational success and how to avoid organizational failure. It must be about an ongoing effort to structure the public sector's institutions into a more productive whole. It must be about the outcomes produced by the indispensable institutions of government. Nothing else will do.

Endnotes

1   David Deutsch, *The Beginning of Infinity* (New York: Viking, 2011), Kindle edition, Section 8017-19.

2   Drucker, *Management*, 353.

About the Author

Richard Clay Wilson, Jr. was a local government manager and executive for thirty-eight years. He was city manager of the City of Santa Cruz, California, for twenty-nine of those years. He retired in 2010 to concentrate on writing about management in the public sector. He holds a bachelor's degree in political science from the University of California at Santa Barbara (1968) and a master's degree in public administration from the University of Kansas (1976).

His account of the 1989 Loma Prieta Earthquake, *The Loma Prieta Earthquake: What One City Learned,* was published by the International City Management Association in 1992. He has also spoken widely about disaster preparedness and recovery to local government audiences.

Wilson lives in Santa Cruz, California, with his wife, Jill, who works at her estate planning law practice. Their son and daughter live and work in New York and Washington, D.C., respectively, so trips to the East Coast are frequent.

CPSIA information can be obtained at www.ICGtesting.com
Printed in the USA
LVOW01s2114190514

386433LV00021B/578/P

9 781626 523388